The Pluricentricity Debate

This book unpacks a 30-year debate about the pluricentricity of German. It examines the concept of pluricentricity, an idea implicit to the study of World Englishes, which expressly allows for national standard varieties, and the notion of "pluri-areality", which seeks to challenge the former. Looking at the debate from three angles—methodological, theoretical and epistemological—the volume draws on data from German and English, with additional perspectives from Dutch, Luxembourgish, Swedish, Danish and Norwegian, to establish if and to what degree "pluri-areality" and pluricentricity model various sociolinguistic situations adequately. Dollinger argues that "pluri-areality" is synonymous with "geographical variation" and, as such, no match for pluricentricity. Instead, "pluri-areality" presupposes an atheoretical, supposedly "neutral", data-driven linguistics that violates basic science–theoretical principles. Three fail-safes are suggested—the uniformitarian hypothesis, Popper's theory of falsification and speaker attitudes—to avoid philological incompatibilities and terminological clutter. This book is of particular interest to scholars in sociolinguistics, World Englishes, Germanic languages and linguists more generally.

Stefan Dollinger is Associate Professor at UBC Vancouver, specializing in historical linguistics, sociolinguistics and linguistic border studies. He is the author of *New-Dialect Formation in Canada* (2008), *The Written Questionnaire in Social Dialectology* (2015) and *Creating Canadian English* (2019), and Chief Editor of the *Dictionary of Canadianisms on Historical Principles*—www.dchp.ca/dchp2 (2017).

The Pluricentricity Debate

On Austrian German and other
Germanic Standard Varieties

Stefan Dollinger

Routledge
Taylor & Francis Group

LONDON AND NEW YORK

First published 2019
by Routledge
2 Park Square, Milton Park, Abingdon, Oxon OX14 4RN
605 Third Avenue, New York, NY 10017

First issued in paperback 2020

Routledge is an imprint of the Taylor & Francis Group, an informa business

Library of Congress Cataloging-in-Publication Data
A catalog record for this book has been requested

ISBN 13: 978-0-367-72884-7 (pbk)
ISBN 13: 978-0-367-14357-2 (hbk)

Typeset in Times New Roman
by Apex CoVantage, LLC

Contents

Tables

Figures

Preface

This book highlights a development in German dialectology that I have noticed with increasing unease over the past few years. It stresses what seems to be missing from the debate about Austrian German and how this national variety is linguistically modelled. By placing German in the context of other Germanic languages, it is my hope that the incompatibilities will become clearer.

This book identifies the problems and proposes ways to redress them. It argues that sociolinguistic concepts that have proven themselves in an international context must be the basis for exploration and elaboration, not new coinages. This book makes the case against a "special status" of German and hopes to bring a theoretical angle into a discussion that has stalled for more than 20 years.

As a linguist and a language teacher, I think that whatever we do as linguists must benefit the speakers and learners of the varieties we deal with. If some of our findings have the potential to go against perceived speaker needs, it is time to take stock and see if a major principle was violated. I believe that in German dialectology we have reached that point in what has been called the "problem" of national varieties. This book contains little new data; its novelty lies in the weaving together of arguments that are usually buried in data-driven presentations; in the combination, juxtaposition and comparison of studies not usually read together.

This book's focus is on theoretical bases and interpretations, how we can know what we know. The new data that is now part of this book was included at the brilliant suggestion of one of two anonymous reviewers in the spring of 2018. I hope the book will be critiqued for its factual points and not, as the clearance reader in early 2019 flippantly accused me of bias, labelling the present book as "not publishable", as written, "from the perspective of an Austrian more concerned about his linguistic identity, than as an academic soberly gauging the debate". Even if that were the case, which it is not, the arguments herein have an intrinsic value. Nobody should be asked to separate their social and linguistic identities. How would this be possible, respectively, and what kind of sociolinguistics would we be getting? Perhaps this is a key question for "pluri-arealists" to answer. When I occasionally refer to the German provenance of colleagues, I do so as a last resort in order to understand why, by virtue of a different kind of socialization and training perhaps, a given view might be so different from the one in the present book.

Not everyone will agree with every point raised, and others will miss some; I felt unable to offer any more depth within the scope of a short monograph. I particularly regret the deletion of the original quotes from the German in footnotes (some 4000 words), as a hard word limit was enforced. I hope to have given just enough context for everyone to allow the arguments to be tested in their own linguistic contexts, so that they may attempt to falsify, in the sense introduced in Section 6.2 and not by categorical dismissal, the account offered herein.

sd

Vancouver, 6 February 2019

Acknowledgements

I owe thanks to many colleagues who answered questions in relation to this book between early 2016 and its publication, or offered **(considerable)** feedback in some form: **Leiv Egil Breivik**, Winifred Davies, **Rudolf de Cillia**, David Crystal, **Martin Durrell**, Christa Dürscheid, Stephan Elspaß, Andrea Ender, Gavin Falconer, Hanna Fischer, Stephan Gaisbauer, **Manfred Glauninger**, John Kirk, Alexandra Lenz, **Mats Mobärg**, **Rudolf Muhr**, **Simon Pickl**, Edgar Platen, **Heinz-Dieter Pohl**, **Jutta Ransmayr**, Gijsbert Rutten, **Herbert Schendl**, Hannes Scheutz, Regula Schmidlin, **Richard Schrodt**, **Peter Trudgill**, Wim Vandenbussche, Michelle Waldispühl, **Ruth Wodak** and Arne Ziegler.

Their naming or highlighting here implies no endorsement of any part of my argument.

Terminological Note

While English terminology is used throughout this book, I aimed to translate all German terms and concepts as faithfully as possible into (international) English. The use of terms such as "German German"—for the German used in Germany—or "Dutch Dutch"—in opposition to "Belgian Dutch"—is in line with Trudgill's terminology (e.g. 2004). I see no problem with such "double" names, though some find them objectionable on aesthetic grounds; they can easily be replaced by, e.g. Deutschland German for German German or Netherlandic Dutch for Dutch Dutch.

1   The Problem

Linguists have for a long time been exploring the idea of language universals. In most cases, such universals are conceived as part of linguistic structure, the inner "mechanics" of the language system. It is therefore somewhat rarer that linguists envisage social universals, despite sociolinguists having established a fair number of consistent behaviours. The present book takes a look at an area of sociolinguistic inquiry pertaining to the treatment of what are often called "non-dominant varieties" of a language. Such varieties include Canadian English, vs. the dominant varieties of American English and British English, or Austrian German vs. German German and Belgian Dutch vs. Dutch Dutch. There are different ways to treat such varieties. In German, for instance, national varieties are often considered a "problem" (e.g. Ammon 1995: subtitle), while in English no such perception exists. A comparison of German and English in this regard is therefore at the core of this book, with five other Germanic languages—Dutch, Luxembourgish, Norwegian, Swedish and Danish—thrown into the mix.

The present book argues that linguistic concepts need to be applicable across various languages and philologies in order to be meaningful. If we are to make lasting progress, we need to have clarity with regards to basic terms, concepts and notions. Every bi- or multilingual student of more than one philology will have noticed a certain dissonance within the concepts of any given language when compared to similar concepts in another language. I argue that linguists should accept a competing concept only if there are very compelling reasons to treat any given language differently.

Recent years have seen the use of a competing concept called "pluri-areality" in German dialectology. "Pluri-areality" and pluri-areal are my renderings from the original German "pluriareale Sprache"—pluri-areal language (Wolf 1994: 74; Scheuringer 1996). "Pluri-areality" directly contradicts the established concept of pluricentricity in its fundamental assumptions of how national varieties are to be modelled. Pluricentricity refers to the development of multiple standards, often national standards of a given language, while "pluri-areality" downplays, if not negates, any national level. The two approaches will be discussed and contrasted in detail.

There may, of course, be very good reasons for using different concepts in different philologies. An area where different cross-linguistic terms are fully justified, even desirable, concerns the various languages' tense systems. How the natural phenomenon of time is split, dissected and mapped onto different tenses varies from language to language. To take a simple example, the French *l'imparfait* is not precisely the same as the German *Mitvergangenheit* (*Präteritum* ["preterite"]) or the English *Past Simple*. The different terms make sense, as they mark different conceptualizations as mirrored in grammar.

But what are linguists supposed to do if they notice different terms and concepts employed for what might reasonably be deemed analogous social situations? This short monograph argues that the modelling of German varieties does not warrant the special term "pluri-areality", a term contradicting the standard international concept of pluricentricity. My argument concerns the areas of dialectology and sociolinguistics, which have a trickling down effect on how we conceptualize what we call the German language in our teaching models. The simple question at the base of this book is whether we accept modelling standard varieties of German differently from standard varieties of English, Danish–Swedish–Norwegian, Spanish or Portuguese, to name but a few.

Professional linguistics has not been immune to isolationist tendencies. Modern language studies—our philologies—have their roots in late eighteenth- and early nineteenth-century nationalist ideals of nation and state, of a discursively constructed *Volk*, a people, and its connection to the imagined but very powerful idea of nation. One can argue that we only talk about languages such as German and French as a result of the political and social developments from that era, developments that are rooted in the idea of the nation. We don't talk about *Occitan* and *Provençal* or *Bavarian* and *Prussian*, but of *French* and *German* as languages for the simple reason that the advocates for French and German were politically stronger than those for Occitan and Provençal or Bavarian and Prussian. As we will see later, the latter have successfully adopted the term "German" (Deutsch) for what might just as well have been called *Prussian*.

At the centre of the argument are some fundamental questions of intellectual inquiry, such as why we use the terms and concepts we use, how we use them and how we know what we think we know about languages and their speakers. In a recent paper, Martin Haspelmath writes that we do not appreciate and value the cross-checking and replication of results enough, as we generally prefer to study new phenomena instead. "Cumulativity and replicability are not much emphasized by linguists", he writes and speculates that these two key features of inquiry "seem difficult to achieve" because "we cannot even agree what we mean by our technical terms" (2019: 83). Two such technical terms are at the centre of this book. The concept of "pluricentricity", as defined by Clyne (1995) and Ammon (1995), and the term "pluri-areality", as first used by Wolf (1994) and Scheuringer (1996).

The concept of "pluri-areality" has been presented as an alternative concept to pluricentricity since the mid-1990s (e.g. Scheuringer 1996; Pohl 1997). German as a Second Language books, however, have increasingly been adopting the pluricentric framework and, with it, the study of national varieties and multiple standards (see e.g. Schmidlin 2011: 86–87). It's only in the past five to ten years that major linguistic proponents have started to reject the established pluricentric model (e.g. Elspaß, Dürscheid & Ziegler 2017; Koppensteiner & Lenz 2016; Dürscheid & Elspaß 2015; Elspaß & Niehaus 2014; Glauninger 2013). As a result, today we may speak of a pluricentricity debate in German. It is hoped that the present account can contribute to its resolution.

1.1 What Is Pluricentricity?

The concept of pluricentricity has been explored and developed in German linguistics in both breadth and scope since the early 1980s. Among the many theoretical and practical contributions to this concept, the monographs and collections by Michael Clyne (1984, 1995), Ulrich Ammon (1995) and their application in the *Dictionary of German Linguistic Variants* (Ammon et al. 2004, 2016) stand out. The *Dictionary* documents the major variants in the German-speaking countries in a pluricentric framework that, above all, rest on the distributions of forms in D (Germany), A (Austria) and CH (Switzerland), the three major national varieties of standard German, the "DACH" varieties. An important predecessor is Heinz Kloss (1952, 1967, 1978, 1993), to be discussed in section 2.4. Pluricentric claims and predictions have in addition been empirically tested in Schmidlin (2011) and Pfrehm (2007), and most recently in de Cillia and Ransmayr (forthcoming).

What is pluricentricity? Pluricentricity is an application of the concept of pluricentric languages. Ammon defines as a pluricentric language as a language that

> is used in more than one country as a national or regional official language if such use has resulted in differences in the standard variety.
> (Ammon et al. 2016: xxxix)[1]

While the official status of a language (as in a constitution or in laws) contributes to the shaping of a pluricentric language, it is no requirement.

In the present book we follow Clyne's definition, which is rooted in Kloss' cross-linguistic anthropological work. Clyne foregrounds the factors of language use, perception and attitudinal features in varieties that have developed norms, whether they are codified—entered in dictionaries and grammars—or not (yet). In Clyne's words, a pluricentric language is defined as follows:

> German, like English, French, Swahili, Spanish, Arabic, Bengali, Chinese and other languages, is an instance of what Kloss (1978: 66–7) terms a "pluricentric" language, i.e. a language with several interacting centres, each providing a national variety with at least some of its own (codified) norms.
>
> (Clyne 1995: 20)

This concept has been applied to some 50 languages in the world to date (e.g. Muhr 2016a, 2016b) and has been tied to the development of codified standard varieties as the major reference point for varieties that are considered as belonging to the same language.

1.2 What Is Pluri-Areality?

If you don't favour pluricentricity, what concept might replace it? Current anti-pluricentrists employ the term "pluri-areality". The 1990s saw a heated debate between mostly Austrian linguists over the state of Austrian German. The two main proponents were Rudolf Muhr, who has been arguing for pluricentricity (e.g. Muhr 1983, 1989, 1996, 2017), and Hermann Scheuringer (1990b, 1996), who rejected the notion as of 1990. The term pluri-areal is defined negatively, in opposition to the pluricentric model, because, as Wolf states:

> Also as an Austrian I argue, at least in light of the state of debate currently, that there exists no "Austrian German" as a uniform variety, because even within Austria—like in the entire German-speaking area—several dialect zones need to be distinguished.
>
> (Wolf 1994: 75)

The term pluri-areal is supposed to reflect a foregrounding of "variation", of historically older dialect zones at the expense of a uniform approach, in the study of standard Austrian German. The remainder of the book will be spent on untangling the assumptions behind such statements to show that they are rooted in a misunderstanding of the concept of pluricentricity. Before a new generation of German scholars picked up and revived the dormant term, "pluri-areality" was a fringe term, a term that remains virtually unknown outside of German linguistics but central to many if not most dialectological approaches of German today.

There are social implications to a rejection of the pluricentric notion. The denial of the legitimacy of non-dominant standard varieties, as lined out by Wolf above, for instance, might be considered as a "neo-colonial" take on German. Charges of colonialism lie heavily, especially in this age when western cultures are beginning to realize the long-term effects of colonization that require reconciliatory action. I do *not* accuse my colleagues of such motivation, but some of their reconceptualizations are reminiscent of such ideas of dominance. Going back to Wolf's (1994) book review that apparently coined "pluri-areality", we see contradictions from the start. Wolf concedes that

> certainly, many speakers within Austria and abroad are aware of an "Austrian German".

But Wolf goes on to "overrule" this conceded speaker awareness, referring to the absence of clear categories:

> It is not just the linguists, however, who have difficulties to specify what precisely constitutes this Austrian German.
>
> (Wolf 1994: 74–75)

It is strange that the concept that is supposed to replace the well-established notion of pluricentricity is introduced as a side remark in Wolf's book review; it is even stranger, however, that the new term has not undergone theoretical or applied explication since.

The pluri-areal approach is characterized by a strict division of the linguistic and the social, with clear primacy given to the former. This begs the question of what kind of sociolinguistics we can expect from such an approach. What my account questions is whether the possibility exists to "just" work objectively on a language. It will be shown that the pluri-areal school is more heavily invested in a language planning paradigm than its statements to the strict separation of language description and language planning suggest.

1.3 Pluricentricity in the World

While Germanic languages are the focus of this volume, the vitality of the pluricentric concept is seen in many languages. In the international context, pluricentricity is at times actively discussed, such as in Spanish (Paffey 2012), Italian (Cerruti, Crocco & Marzo 2017), or Portuguese (Mendes et al. 2014). Even French, which often counts as the paradigm case of a language that does not tolerate much variation, is now increasingly viewed as a pluricentric language. Kircher (2012: 363) finds evidence among "more favourable attitudes towards QF", Quebec French, among francophones, showing that a "preference for QF on the solidarity dimension" (ibid.: 365) is detectable today.

It seems that a pluricentric perspective develops quite naturally as an effect of the intricate connection of language and identity. Such identities can be suppressed for a while, but they cannot be controlled. Catalan speakers, for instance, were considered speakers of non-standard dialects for much of the twentieth century. Most actively suppressed by the Franco regime, Catalans themselves did not accept this status for their variety. Today, two generations after Franco's reign, Catalan is more or less accepted, and speakers "consider their mother-tongue a full-fledged language" (Kloss 1993: 165). The question is how long others can deny such status to Catalan more generally. And who can argue with the speakers of Catalan? It is indeed hard to imagine a linguist who explains to Catalan speakers that, based on some abstract criterion, they are "wrong" and should abandon their claims to linguistic independence.

A notable development is the formation of a conference series dedicated to the study of non-dominant varieties of languages. These conferences, organized by the Working Group of Non-Dominant Languages, have been hosted in a number of countries since 2011 and have addressed the pluricentricity of four to five dozen languages, from Albanian, Aymara, Arabic, Aramaic and Armenian via Guarani, Hausa, Hebrew, Hindi, Hokkien to Tamil, Tamazight/Berber and Urdu (pluricentriclanguages.org). Their conference proceedings (Muhr 2012, and most recently in Muhr 2016a, 2016b) show the appeal and vitality of the pluricentric concept as the established standard in the modelling of national varieties.

1.4 Pluricentricity in the Germanic Languages

As the previous section demonstrates, a focus on a few select Germanic languages is arbitrary yet practical. While the following discussion is relevant for possibly any language that has developed a standardized form of some kind, contrasting the contexts and scholarly debates in the languages of German, English, Dutch, Swedish/Danish/Norwegian and Luxembourgish exposes a number of fault lines that might otherwise remain hidden.

These seven Germanic languages are different and alike at the same time. There is the "big" German language, a language that has taken a reputational hit in the twentieth century, so much so that it has given rise to an entirely new standard language (Luxembourgish) and new standard varieties (Austrian German, Swiss German). There is the "very big" English language, the most international language in the world of today, a language with many more non-native speakers than native speakers; in this respect alone, English is different from the other languages mentioned here. There is Dutch, which, as far as its setting in Europe is concerned, might be on the brink of creating a second standard variety of Dutch (in addition to Afrikaans, which is considered an independent language). Finally, there are the Northern Germanic standard languages: Danish, Swedish and Norwegian, all mutually intelligible, often more so than some varieties of German, yet they are considered independent languages. Especially Norwegian offers an important scenario of the way a new standard variety, in this case a new language, can develop in a very short time.

The focus on these Germanic languages affords the book a purposeful, minimally cross-linguistic focus that allows central issues to come into the foreground, while still staying within the tight constraints of a short monograph. Most of this book will focus on German and English, as the two most extreme cases of how national varieties may be modelled and treated. While the definition of pluricentric languages uses the terms country or nation, there is no theoretical a priori requirement for such entities to be involved. What is required is that the language in question is used in more than one location, with a communicative network and discourse communities that are sufficiently independent but not isolated from one another.

"Locations" for the Germanic languages may be nations, although there are a number of Germanic languages that do not have such institutional backing. Frisian, Yiddish and Plattdeutsch are in no such fortunate position, for instance. Since the same processes apply to these as to state-supported languages, a centre is *not* to be a priori equated with a nation or nation state. In this context, Clyne speaks of full centres (the DACH countries for German), half centres (Liechtenstein, Luxembourg, South Tyrol and Eastern Belgium), and even quarter centres (e.g. Namibia as a former German colony or Mennonite communities in North America). In other words, while countries are no prerequisite for pluricentricity, practically they are often the entities that can most effectively support such linguistic diversification.

It is easy, in fact, to think of examples where linguistic centres are not fully independent countries, such as Scotland (with Scots, a Germanic language) and Scottish English within the United Kingdom (McColl Millar 2005), or the German-speaking parts of Belgium (Küpper, Leuschner & Rothstein 2017) or Southern Tyrol, the latter including a de facto standard variety by speakers socialized within the Italian state. For all intents and purposes, however, nation states generally offer infrastructure, media and other channels to reinforce nation-wide communication networks, so much so that they may be assumed to constitute linguistic full centres—centres that support a national variety in most if not all aspects. This congruence of nations with full linguistic centres is an often misconstrued point (e.g. Glauninger 2013: 125–126).

For the Germanic languages discussed here, different degrees of adoption of the pluricentric model can be discerned. Swedish, Norwegian and Danish on the one hand, and Luxembourgish on the other, all left the spectrum of national varieties of one language and have gone the route of independent languages for socio-political, not linguistic, reasons. German and, as we will see, European Dutch seem to be pluricentrically more restrictive, with German on the extreme end promoting "pluri-areality" instead of pluricentricity. English, of course, is on the spectrum's opposite end, with more national varieties than any other language to date (see, e.g. Kortmann et al. 2004; Schneider et al. 2004; Kortmann & Luckenheimer 2011).

The way English linguists construe pluricentricity is the antithesis of its treatment by a substantial number of German linguists. In English, there is often little explicit discussion about pluricentricity: it is implicitly accepted and not questioned. It is, as it were, part of the DNA of English linguistics, which is reflected in statements such as the "truism that English is nowadays a pluricentric language" (Hickey 2012: 22). Pluricentricity is so engrained into the fabric of English that entire disciplines are built on it. It underpins the study of World Englishes, the pedigree of which dates back at least to the 1950s (e.g. Partridge & Clark 1951; Avis 1954). Today, English linguistics without a strong pluricentric element is unimaginable, as is the return to the exclusive study of English English and American English (e.g. Watts & Trudgill 2002). Without pluricentricity, Kachru's model of World Englishes (Kachru 1985), Peter Trudgill's (2004) *New-Dialect Formation Model* and Edgar Schneider's *Dynamic Model* (2007) would be unthinkable.

The usefulness of pluricentricity is overwhelming in the English context and indeed the international context. Such fact, of course, does not mean that the concept is correct. It merely demonstrates the accepted opinion of linguists worldwide. If this way of modelling language varieties is wrong, however, all these approaches would be wrong, too. That seems unlikely, though not impossible.

Is German really different? Is it different enough to warrant its own counter concept? We might ask how far any "special status" of a given philology may be pushed: should German be treated differently than English, and ultimately the other Germanic languages, including those that have gone on to become independent languages? A reasonable stance appears to be that some linguistic structures, the *l'imparfait* vs. *simple past*, will likely be philology-dependent. The terms and concepts that govern the sociolinguistic structure of related languages, such as the Germanic ones, however, won't be. Sociolinguistic terms and concepts that are applied to only one setting should remain the clear exception, and one would first ask if anything in the modelling of that particular context had been overlooked.

1.5 An Outline of the Book

This book's structure is as follows: Chapter 2 introduces and defines basic terms and concepts. Chapters 3 and 4 present the international way of modelling national varieties and the "German" way. Chapter 3 deals with English, Danish–Norwegian–Swedish, Belgian Dutch and Dutch as well as Luxembourgish, which are all languages and varieties viewed in the framework of pluricentricity, with the possible exception of European Dutch, where the next few years should show which model will prevail. Chapter 4 is dedicated to the "German" model of "pluri-areality". Chapters 5 and 6 then attempt to falsify, in Popper's sense, both the pluricentric and the pluri-areal approach. As will become clear, the section against pluricentricity inevitably turns into a critique of the pluri-areal critique. Chapter 7 then presents a key point, new speaker attitude data on Austrian German and key concepts such as linguistic insecurity. It makes the point that "pluri-arealists", despite their criticism of language planning, do in fact themselves engage in language planning to their own liking. Chapter 8 offers four examples from Austrian German of what the "pluri-arealists" disregard, before Chapter 9 suggests three safeguards against the adoption of theoretically and descriptively "empty" concepts, such as "pluri-areality".

Note

1 Most quotations have been translated from the German. All translations are by the present book's author and strive to render the meanings. Due to strict space constraints, the originals can unfortunately not be provided here.

2 Standardizing German
Concepts and Background

A special problem in German is the existence of more than the customary binary distinction into standard and non-standard. As Pedersen (2005: 174) reminds us, "standardization is an ongoing process", and there is, in many accounts today, a third variety that is the everyday koiné, a compromise variety between formal and informal styles, which is neither traditional dialect nor formal standard. In Table 2.1, this middle-of-the-road koiné in German is called "Umgangssprache" or "Alltagssprache", while an English term might be "colloquial standard".

Umgangssprache is perhaps comparable with newer developments in English, such as Estuary English, i.e. the adoption of traditional lower-class variants by socially privileged speakers and the creation of, for instance, an urban language variety that is less formal than the standard but more formal than the working-class or traditional dialects. In some languages, such as Italian, a colloquial standard has developed that tolerates, as in Standard British English, the use of regional accents with the codified standard (Cerruti, Crocco & Marzo 2017: 7).

The assignment of linguistic items to any one stylistic level, in German "Sprachschichten", is a notorious problem. While standard German "as an idea enjoys a high level of support", "there is substantial disagreement over the concrete form of this variety" in Germany (Davies 2009: 204), let alone in Austria or Switzerland. One problem seems to be speaker knowledge, exposure and attitude. The outsider to a group often labels everything "odd to their ears" as non-standard, thus de-valuing Standard Austrian German constructions as non-standard. Conversely, Austrians, like many other speakers of non-dominant varieties, have been socialized with feelings of linguistic insecurity and inferiority, much like the speakers of Belgian Dutch. As we will see in section 3.3.1, in the post-World War II period, the Flemish were expressly taught an exonormative standard as the target norm.

In this book, no ontological distinction is made between language, variety or dialect, as they are linguistically equivalent as social constructs. "Standard" means the codified norm of a language variety: codified in dictionaries

Table 2.1 Barbour and Stevenson's "Sprachschichten"

German terminology	English terminology	Barbour and Stevenson
Standardsprache ("standard lg") Elnheitssprachc ("unified lg") Schriftsprache ("written lg") Literatursprachc ("literary lg")	standard language	formal standard
Umgangssprache		colloquial standard "Hochdeutsch"
Alltagssprache "colloquial language"	(non-standard) Dialect	colloquial non-standard
Dialekt Mundart		traditional dialect

Source: Barbour and Stevenson (1990: 141)

and grammars and accepted to a given degree in the population. As such, standard language is used "to denote a process of more or less conscious, and centralized regulation of language" (Weinreich 1954: 396). "Standard" is different from "norm": while the former is codified, the latter is an expression of majority usage. If one limits the range of speakers and writers to those that display "model character", such as TV news anchors and major national and regional newspapers, their use would offer a "colloquial standard" or a de facto behavioural standard. Such standard, also called Gebrauchsstandard, should find its reflection in the language codex, i.e. the codified language in dictionaries and grammars.

Norms can be behavioural in one's linguistic choices or evaluative in one's assessments of linguistic behaviour. The major finding of the famous New York City and Norwich studies by Labov and Trudgill have shown "that speech communities show a uniform set of evaluative norms" (Labov 2001: 213). It is the evaluation, not the linguistic behaviour per se, that makes a speech community. Like any larger communities, national speech communities are generally imagined. While descriptive linguists work with model speakers and model texts to describe the colloquial standard, there is no single speaker that fully lives the codified standard. Codified standards are the result of imagined linguistic behaviour and express a standard-language mindset, as Pedersen reminds us:

> Standard languages are founded on the belief that varieties other than the selected one are wrong. This proscription goes hand in hand with codification, operating as a "standard ideology", and often having a strong influence on speakers' attitudes and linguistic behaviour.
> (Pedersen 2005: 172)

Using Labov's definition, we define speech community not as a community that shares linguistic behaviour but one that shares the linguistic evaluation of features, which includes shared pejorative or negative views of one's variety. This means that Austrian speakers of German or Luxembourg speakers of German who feel insecure about their German show by their evaluative agreement alone just as much positive evidence for the existence of a national speech community as, say, speakers in Hanover or Hamburg who feel good about their German and their speech community. In other words, if Flemish speakers consider Flemish dialects as "lacking" in some way or another, their shared agreement co-constitutes their speech community of Flemish speakers.

While sociolinguists have traditionally focused on non-standard urban varieties and dialectologists on traditional non-standard dialects, standard varieties, too, are socially relevant. Labov uses Bourdieu to state that if

> control of the standard language is viewed as a basic form of symbolic capital (Bourdieu 1980), then sociolinguistic stratification is the result of the differential ability of speakers to produce the standard forms and inhibit the nonstandard forms.
>
> (Labov 2001: 105)

Control over standard varieties is therefore a question of social power. Widdowson (1994) has shown in the debate over a global standard of English that the stakes are high, which also applies to control over standards in the Germanic varieties discussed here. Lastly, it is important to know that a formal standard variant, which is by our definition a codified variant, can but often does not match the local "behavioural norm, i.e. majority behaviour" or the colloquial standard.

2.1 Contiguous Borders vs. Sea Borders

English linguistics has maintained for the better part of a century that national varieties of English are useful constructs. The antecedents of the idea that nations serve as a relevant category in English language development go back to the beginning of codification of American English in the late eighteenth century. American English is, of course, no homogenous entity; it is rich with variation (see e.g. Labov, Ash & Boberg 2005), yet its standard variety, like any standard variety, is fairly uniform by comparison. The development of an American standard did not happen overnight; throughout the nineteenth century, what was to become known as Standard American English would often be ridiculed as uncivilized and rude.

The situation in German may appear to be different because of the coincidental fact that the nations in which German is the dominant language share land borders. As Figure 2.1 shows, German-language borders are contiguous.

By contrast, the Inner Circle Englishes, i.e. those Englishes that have been derived from native speakers, are geographically defined by sea borders, with the exception of two international borders; these are the Canada–US and the UK–Irish border in Northern Ireland. The English–Scottish border, the linguistically most diverse border in the English-speaking Inner Circle, is currently politically a regional, internal border, yet it shows all the trappings of dividing two linguistic centres—a Scots and Scottish English centre and an English English centre (e.g. Watt, Llamas & Johnson 2010; Llamas, Watt & Johnson 2009).

What seems like an obvious choice in English may not have seemed as obvious in the post-war German-speaking countries. In the interwar period, Austrians were considering themselves by and large as "linguistically German" (Wiesinger 2000: 543), so that linguistic differences were at that time not well suited to be socially indexed as Austrian. With the exception of some Austrian patriots in the period, such as Carl Friedrich Hrauda (1948 [1938]), it was only after 1945 that an Austrian identity was carved out of the destruction of World War II, an identity that included linguistic aspects,

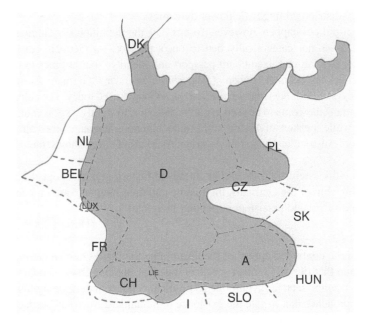

Figure 2.1 German-speaking area (dark) in Europe and state boundaries

Source: Maas (2014: 40)

some of which had been documented "over the time frame of half a century" by Wollmann (1948: 365) who offers perhaps the best characterization of Standard Austrian German at that point in time, dealing with all linguistic levels.

2.2 What's in a Name?

Members of dominant nations often come to see their varieties as the default norms, the "unmarked" varieties, out of habit. English speakers in the American state of Michigan, for instance, consider themselves "accent free" (Preston 1998: 142) and think themselves model speakers. The term "General American", based on the allegedly unmarked speech in the Midwest, was therefore replaced with the concept of Standard American English (Kretzschmar 2008).

The matching names of the German language and German nationality support similar self-stylizations of the "real" German only to be found in Germany. Schmidlin (2011: 88) refers in this context to the idea of a "continuity phantasy" in which the linguistic history of German is equated with the history of Germany. Ammon (1995: 323) surmised that if Prussian-led Germany had adopted a name like Great Prussia rather than Germany, such confusion would not have come about. In that case, Great Prussians, Austrians and Swiss would speak German, which might have resulted in more evenly distributed linguistic power dynamics.

That did not happen, however. To this day, the definition of "German"—*deutsch*—is not categorically tied to one's passport—a German, Austrian, Italian, Belgian or Luxembourg passport and identity—but at times to one's language—a German Italian (*Deutschitaliener*) or "German Austrian" (*Deutschösterreicher*), though the latter is no longer used today. The adjective "Austrian" has come to be used in public discourse to signify a speaker of German, while speakers of Austria's other autochthonous languages are defined as Romani Austrian or Hungarian Austrian. As Martin Durrell shows, the

> myths established by earlier linguistic historiography about the relationship of the Germans, their name and their language are immensely powerful and persistent in popular imagination.
>
> (Durrell 2009: 183)

Given the continued appeal of the idea of one Standard German German, a German that ties all German speakers together, the ONE STANDARD GERMAN AXIOM can be seen as an unreflected political concept underpinning linguistic approaches that negate the existence of a Standard Austrian German.

The idea that German German variants are "default" and unmarked is widespread even in linguistic circles. Ammon (1995: 375) reports that in the 1990s there was hardly any awareness ("kaum [. . .] Bewußtsein") about the existence of Germanisms (Teutonisms), "partially also among linguists who were working on German as a pluricentric language". Also, literati are prone to German hegemony. The late Wendelin Schmidt-Dengler, doyen of Austrian Literature, once reported a conversation with a young literary critic from a well-known Hamburg weekly, who remarked that

> Austrian literature today is something that always includes a cow barn, a noose and a suicide—on top of everything being very Catholic. In some sense it is even worse than what one would expect in Bavaria.
>
> (Schmidt-Dengler 1995: 38)

The quip is used here because Schmidt-Dengler found it relevant to share it in a collection on Austrian German, indicating that he considered the attitude as a quite typical one that should be overcome.

A related onomastic question concerns the naming of Austrian German. Is it called "German in Austria" or "Austrian German"? Schneider's "Dynamic Model" ties the most crucial elements of the formation of a new standard variety to phase 4 in his 5-phase model, which he calls endonormative standardization. Schneider states that the

> difference between phases 3 and 4 is commonly given symbolic expression by substituting a label of the "English in X" type by a newly coined "X English".
>
> (Schneider 2007: 50)

In this context, "German in Austria" can be seen as a programmatic announcement in opposition to "Austrian German". As Schneider continues:

> The former marks the dialect as just a variant without a discrete character of its own, while the latter credits it with the status of a distinct type, set apart and essentially on equal terms with all others.
>
> (Schneider 2007: 50)

Pluri-areal interpretations have recently demoted Austrian German to "German in Austria". Seifter and Seifter are most extreme in their denial of an independent Austrian variety of German, as their reaction to the Austrian Minister of Education's promotion of an information booklet on Austrian German illustrates:

> Much of this language-political guide for apparently correct German instruction can be considered as political indoctrination. Such clumsy attempt at influence is not only dispensable, but dangerous in an education system that is rooted in the responsibility of the individual, the

support of democratic principles that aims "to promote the readiness for independent thinking and critical self-reflection".

(Seifter & Seifter 2016: 42)

The charge of "political indoctrination" is bizarre given the minister's mandate to support the students' awareness of and education in a standard variety that is relevant in the Austrian context. While every person is free to choose a linguistic model, in a school environment anything but the use of Austrian norms would not serve the students.

2.3 The Standardization of Written German

The standardization of German went basically in lock-step with other European languages. By the late eighteenth century, a universally shared written German standard was a beginning fact. The idea of the unity of the spoken German varieties was developed at the time, too. In contradiction to persisting variation, language has since served as an ideological marker of "Germanness" (Durrell 2017: 24). Beginning in the 1450s, the European states were engaged in nation building. Mattheier (2003: 219) stresses the importance "for the socio-cultural development of the territory to have a language that could function as an instrument of national identification". The original identification process was to unify all German speakers in what is now Germany, Switzerland, Austria, Belgium, Luxembourg, Czechia and Italy under Austrian leadership, as the Habsburgs were Emperors of the Holy Roman Empire of the German Nation. In line with these aspirations, a "southern Imperial standard" (ibid.: 218) was used since Emperor Maximilian I (1459–1519) in Vienna, a standard that came to be known as "Gemeindeutsch" or "Common German".

At around the same time, an East Central German standard (ECG), based in the Duchy of Saxony, developed as a second standard. Martin Luther's bible translations from the 1520s, which were a development of that Saxon standard, further increased that variety's prestige, making ECG and what came to be known as Lutherdeutsch or Meißnerdeutsch (based on the Saxon city of Meißen) the most "elegant", "beautiful", "efficient" and prestigious variety of German. This ECG would steadily exert pressure on other Protestant regions in Germany throughout the sixteenth and seventeenth centuries, leading to its unparalleled acceptance as the written norm in the Protestant parts. Until the mid-1700s, the Imperial Standard was used in Catholic Bavaria, Austria and other southern regions and remained fairly unaffected by ECG.

This was to change in the latter half of the eighteenth century. The age of normative grammars produced two outstanding grammarians, Johann Christoph Gottsched (1700–1766), born in Prussia and working in Leipzig

(Saxony), and Johann Christoph Adelung (1732–1806). Adelung's multi-volume grammar and dictionary (1774–1786) superseded Gottsched's 1748 *Grundlegung der deutschen Sprachkunst* (revised in fifth edition in 1762), which was exclusively based on ECG and northern German writers. Gottsched exerted tremendous influence on the standardization of German based on ECG, which was only further refined by Adelung's more comprehensive work.

Early critics of the ECG standard existed. Vienna's first university professor of German, Johann Siegmund Valentin Popowitsch, argued for a koiné as a standard rather than ECG, choosing the "best" individual forms from the best writers from all German-speaking regions. He therefore critiqued ECG and

> the harmful preconception of Gottsched's followers that the Saxon dialect [ECG] must be regarded as the High German [standard] language.
> (Popowitsch 1780, transl. and quoted in Havinga 2018: 70)

It is significant to note that grammarians before Gottsched considered both the Imperial Standard and ECG as unmarked standards (e.g. Antesperg's grammar from 1734; see Havinga 2018: 48–54).

By the mid-eighteenth century, a discussion ensued about the inappropriateness of the Imperial Standard, which had developed in the southern centres of Vienna (at the Habsburg's imperial court), Augsburg and Nuremberg (Mattheier 2003: 220–221). Empress Maria Theresia, who ruled Austria from 1740–1780, and her more radical reformer son Joseph II (co-regent from 1765, ruling until 1790), played pivotal roles in the reorientation of standardization in Austria (Wiesinger 2000: 528–529). Until that point, the Imperial Standard was noticeably "Austrian" and different from the Saxon Standard. With Maria Theresia's appointment of professors of German at diplomatic academies and universities and, most importantly, the introduction of compulsory education in 1774, one can speak of an "invisibilising" (Havinga 2018) of the Imperial Standard from the late eighteenth century and the adoption of ECG (Mattheier 2003: 221). Adelung's grammar, completed in 1786, is at times seen as the end of the ECG-ization of the Austrian standard.

The eighteenth century also marks the beginning of a founding myth of the German people, which is, as Durrell (2002) shows, rooted in an ethnic-linguistic idea of nation, i.e. a nation state whose members are tied together by a common language. The misconception of a written standard German, a literary German called *Hochdeutsch*, as the original language and the dialects as mere deviations of that ideal is still present today as "its teleology is superficially plausible and aspects of it remarkably persistent" (2002: 93). Empress Maria Theresia clearly saw herself as a German

Empress; after all, she was the leader of the Holy Roman Empire of the German Nation. Consequently, her school reforms show the systematic fight against native Austrian–German constructions, which were coming to be viewed as no longer suitable. With compulsory schooling, Austrian schoolbooks were centrally approved by 1774, and these books promoted the use of ECG. Havinga agrees with Polenz in that ECG "and northern German literature was circulating in the Habsburg Monarchy before the middle of the 18th century", offering a kind of foothold "for Austria's open-mindedness towards the ECG standard, in contrast to the greater conservatism in Bavaria" (2018: 40).

One individual, Johann Ignaz von Felbiger (1724–1788), was implementing the standard reversal in the Empress' name. Felbiger had undergone a personal linguistic reorientation before embarking on reorienting the written Austrian standard. Born in Silesia when it was Austrian to an Austrian father and a Bavarian mother, Felbiger became a "loyal Prussian subject" (Havinga 2018: 73) when Silesia became Prussian in 1742. As educational adviser to the Empress, Felbiger not only recommended compulsory education, but actively prescribed ECG from in his monopoly "textbooks on German language, most of which were published anonymously" with only "a few revisions in line with Adelung's [ECG] norms" (ibid.). In a detailed case study on the loss of e-apocope in the dative, i.e. *der Frau* (native Austrian form) vs. *der Fraue*, or plural *der Fraun* (AUT) vs. *der Frauen*, Havinga concludes "that Felbiger's school reform played a major role in the invisibilisation of e-apocope in reading primers" (ibid.: 220). The "conscious and deliberate stigmatization of linguistic features" (ibid.: 224) did not affect spoken language use, however. Havinga stresses that many of the ECG features remain, to this day, confined to writing and much less so to spoken Austrian German (Havinga 2018: 13).

The acceptance of this new standard, which was "essentially a cultural artefact", was a "puzzling" development that "provided a focus for nationalist aspirations in the 19th century" (Durrell 2002: 99). The early nineteenth century saw the further spread of the ECG written standard, pushing out native features in writing. This brought critical Austrian voices to the fore, including the poet Franz Grillparzer (Scheichl 1996). At that point, native Austrian variants had come to be considered "dialectal" and non-standard (Wiesinger 2000: 534), which showed the effects of a standard that was no longer derived from Austrian varieties.

Since Austria's exclusion from German unification after 1866 and the formation of a *kleindeutsch* ("little-German") unification, the ECG standard can be considered an exonormative standard—a standard to which resistance never fully ceased. Opponents to ECG include prominent Austrian names. In the 1920s, Ludwig Wittgenstein worked for a time as a primary school teacher. He published an elementary school dictionary for use in Austria that

> should include only words that are known to Austrian elementary students. Therefore it excludes many a good German word that are unusual in Austria.
>
> (Wittgenstein 1926: xxvii, qtd. in Scheichl 1926: 148)

Wittgenstein obviously had the goal of delivering an endonormative standard to Austrian students.

The interwar period is often presented as dominated by German unificationist thought in Austria, yet it shows signs of considerable linguistic awareness. Richard Beer-Hoffmann, for instance, wrote about the dilemma of the Austrian writer, who was obligated to write in an exonormative standard. The writer can "either let himself be persuaded that the northern German—not his own language use—is the right one" or to continue to "reject it [the northern German use] internally" but use it anyway "against one's nature" (qtd. in Scheichl 1996: 149). As both options are identity-denying, it should be no surprise that the ECG standard was exposed to critique and ridicule. It is reported that parodies of Standard German German, ECG, became "a sport" in Vienna's theatre scene (Scheichl 1996: 150), which holds to the present day in the context of the Austrian *Kabarett* ("comedy") shows.

The impetus in the wake of German nationalist zeal to wipe out or at least minimize existing variation seems logical though only full-length dictionaries would be able to achieve that goal. The results of the 1st Berlin Orthographic Conference in 1876, with Austria present, were rejected in some German provinces as well as Austria, and länder continued to issue their own orthographic dictionaries. The second Berlin Orthographic Conference, in 1901, devised rules for Germany and Austria and now included Switzerland. These rules were officially adopted and served as a backdrop for orthography until 1996, the date of the latest (modest) reform.

After the second conference, orthographic differences remained largely in the integration of loanwords, where the southern German states continued, against their political affiliation, to follow Austria's lead of integrating loanwords to a much lesser degree than in Prussia (Ammon 1995: 121). It is not insignificant that Ammon suspects the southern German states, Bavaria, Baden, Württemberg as "going with" ("gehen mit") Austrian orthography and not the other way around, as we today often read when there are parallels in Bavaria and Austria.

While bigger states, such as Bavaria and Prussia, as well as Austria, continued to publish their own dictionaries, they adhered to the regulations set out in the joint 1901 document, which Konrad Duden used as the base for revising his own dictionaries. The Duden series would soon be accepted as the de facto standard dictionary for Germany (Polenz 1999: 240). While Duden dictionaries have at least since the 1950s claimed to represent all German-speaking regions, the claim must be "seriously doubted" (Ammon 1995: 365) on account of German German words being presented as the unmarked "standard". In fact, Duden resources have a noticeable ECG and northern German bias.

Because of its history, orthography should be kept aside from other linguistic levels, e.g. lexis, syntax, pronunciation, morphology and pragmatics. The treatment of orthography is different the only salient difference between the standardization of German and English: while the orthography of German has remained unified for some 200 years, English has seen a diversification in that period from one norm into two and more.

2.4 *Abstand, Ausbau* Language and "Roofing"

The terms *ausbau* and *abstand* language, proposed by Heinz Kloss* (1952, 1978), are central to the theory of pluricentricity. The terms label standard varieties as created in one of two ways. The first method, *abstand*, is by virtue of differential linguistic developments over long periods of time. An example would be the differentiation of Western Germanic into modern English and modern German, for instance. This is language differentiation by "linguistic distance" or *abstand*.

The second type of language, *ausbau*, comes about by virtue of language planning and a more active involvement by speaker groups. Examples are the development of Norwegian independently from Danish and Swedish; the codification of Dutch as a standard language in opposition to German; or the creation of a Luxembourgish standard variety from Luxembourg German varieties. This process is called *ausbau*, which may be translated as "differentiation by social development". What appears to be two different processes, linguistic differentiation by "linguistic distance" or by "social development", however, are two sides of the same coin that may and do happen simultaneously.

Some tend to think, some linguists included, that the process of *ausbau* is less authentic than the *abstand* process, but such is not the case when we look at some examples of *ausbau* languages:

> Striking examples [of *ausbau*] are the relations existing between Czech and Slovak, Danish and Swedish, Bulgarian and Macedonian. Of the last-named tongue, H. G. Lunt [. . .] writes: "That Macedonians should accept standard Bulgarian for their own use [or vice versa] would demand far fewer concessions on their part than have been made by

Bavarians and Hamburgers [for accepting standard German German], [or] by Neapolitans and Piedmontese [for accepting standard Italian] [. . .]". There could be no better illustration of what *ausbau* language means.

(Kloss 1993: 161)

Kloss' words make the important point that the *ausbau* process is not in any way less important or common than the *abstand* process. The reason why we speak of different languages and not of varieties of the same language is not that the former are different by any objective measure, but that the socio-political constraints were favourable for such labelling at some point in time, which triggered linguistic changes reinforcing that choice. Chambers and Trudgill consider the distinction of varieties into languages as a linguistic paradox:

> we have to recognize that, paradoxically enough, a "language" is not a particularly linguistic notion at all. Linguistic features obviously come into it, but it is clear that we consider Norwegian, Swedish, Danish and German to be single languages for reasons that are as much political, geographical, historical, sociological and cultural as linguistic.
>
> (Chambers & Trudgill 1998: 4)

This means that we cannot treat varieties that are labelled languages, e.g. German and Dutch, as any different from national varieties of the same language. The latter, just as the former, were in the fact created by some kind of border—political, social, geographical and/or cognitive. Rather than relying on language labels, a focus on the interplay of linguistic varieties and identities would be a more promising approach. This is because Flemish—Belgian Dutch—may be as important, perhaps more so, for the speaker's identity and sense of self, than Dutch is to a Dutch speaker. Especially in an international or global context, such issues tend to come to the fore.

The concept of "roofing" (*Überdachung*) is another useful idea that aligns with linguistic autonomy and heteronomy. The concept specifies the linguistic orientation towards a particular standard. For present-day Norwegian, the roof is Standard Norwegian, while in 1800 that roof would have been Standard Danish. For the Slovaks prior to 1993, the roof would have been the standard Czech of Prague. The concept of roofing is useful as it allows for dynamic assignments and reassignments of reference points as they are negotiated and renegotiated. In pre-1750s Austria, the roofing variety would have been Gemeindeutsch, or the Imperial Standard, while later it would have been East Central German.

The most widely known *ausbau* variety is American English. It is remarkable not just as the first postcolonial variety of English that has run the full course of language development (Schneider 2007), but also because of the important role that just one person, self-trained lexicographer Noah Webster, played in that process. Since 1783, when Webster's first spelling book was published, active tinkering with lexis and orthography has increased the linguistic distance between the American and British standard varieties, with dictionaries in 1806 and 1828 codifying American English. By 1919, when H. L. Mencken published his provocatively entitled *The American Language*, American English was well on its way to becoming a new standard. When the supplements to Mencken's (1936) last edition appeared shortly after World War II in 1945 and 1948, American English was a social fact. Since then, English has had two dominant standard varieties, British English and American English, with the momentum on the latter's side.

Note

* Heinz Kloss made an important contribution to sociolinguistics with his idea of "roofing" in the postwar period, which established the theoretical base of national and other superregional varieties. During World War II, however, he appears to have accepted aspects of National Socialist ideology, something one would not suspect from his post-war writing. His 1944 book, whose title translates as *Statistics, Media, and Organizations of Jewry in the United States and Canada*, which was based on field work in the 1930s in North America, can be read as a demographic map that identifies the Jewish population of North America; a copy of the book, which appears to have come from Hitler's personal library, is held by the National Archives of Canada.

At the core of the present book lies the concept of pluricentricity, which needs to be understood independently of Kloss' apparent acceptance of National Socialist ideas during the Hitler regime, since his post-war work bears no traces of this.

3 The International Pluricentric Model

Standard American English is a reality today. The creation of that standard, however, did not happen overnight and was not a given. American English serves as the oldest example of a fully developed *ausbau* variety, and there are many other national Englishes, such as Canadian English and New Zealand English, but also Indian English, Jamaican English or Bahamian English (see Schneider 2007). Standard American English is the result of language planning and a concerted long-term effort by individuals that was taken up and accepted by the American populace as a linguistic expression of a collective identity.

Noah Webster's famous dictum from 1789 expresses the idea of an American English as a consciously designed artefact:

> As an independent nation, our honor requires us to have a system of our own, in language as well as in government.
> (Webster in 1789, qtd. in Fisher 2001: 62)

What is less known is that Webster came to promote Americanisms only as a second thought. With his first 1783–1785 spelling book, he originally attempted to "enforce uniformity in English worldwide" (Fisher 2001: 62). By the speller's 1787 new edition, however, Webster "had been drawn into the nationalistic movement" (ibid.), emphasizing American differences in his choices. The codification of a second standard variety of standard English, Standard American English, began early and, as Webster's quote above demonstrates, in express opposition to the British standard. This is how some national codification works, as Einar Haugen's time-tested four-tiered process of standardization (1966) has shown.

In late 1782/1783, what would eventually be called *The American Spelling Book and Grammar* was already sold by the dozen (14 pence apiece or 10 shillings a dozen; Daniel 2009: 334, fn 22). According to book historians, Webster's speller became "the most widely read secular book in eighteenth and nineteenth-century America", and by 1818, Webster himself estimated that 5 million copies had been sold (ibid.), an astonishing number in a country of some 9 million people at the time, not even considering the lower literacy rates. This "Blue-Back Speller" was so "amazingly successful", with "total sales of perhaps 100,000,000 copies" (Algeo 2001: 34), that it had the power to instil new norms on the American population in a very short time.

The speller was filling a social and linguistic need that ultimately led to Webster's 1828 *American Dictionary of the English Language* and later to H. L. Mencken's *The American Language* (1919), by which time Standard American English had become a viable alternative to Standard British English. From that point on, there was no turning back the eventual development of other standard varieties in response to changing social conditions. Such developments can be utterly peaceful, e.g. the separation of the British colonies of Jamaica or Belize into statehood.

A particularly good example of a peaceful separation is the division of Czechoslovakia into the Czech Republic and Slovakia in 1993. What used to be Czech dialects in 1992 became Slovak dialects in 1993, though linguistically at first nothing had changed, except the labels and perhaps the speaker's attitudes towards their "languages". Such development is *not* per se a return to the era of nationalism. It is rather the linguistic expression of identities as they change and morph from one instantiation, e.g. Czechoslovak, into another, e.g. Slovak and Czech, that fit a qualified majority of the affected people better. Language labels and orientations change as manifestations of the social aspects of their speakers. What used to be via force—such as the "re-roofing" of the Danish dialects in Skåne into Swedish dialects as of 1658 (Chambers & Trudgill 1998: 10–11)—is now accomplished peacefully via negotiation.

The development of English did not stop with Inner Circle countries, where settler varieties are spoken. Since the 1980s, the former non-settler colonies, i.e. those colonies whose English has been influenced by second-language learning processes, have striven to control and codify their own varieties. These local features have given rise to new national standards (e.g. Bamgbose 1998). This means that former colonies such as India, Pakistan or the Philippines are beginning to take "ownership" of their Englishes (see Widdowson 1994). In the last decade, the call for "ownership" has been heard not just from former second-language colonies, but also from the non-native speakers of English that use English frequently, habitually and comfortably with other non-native speakers, i.e. as a lingua franca. This growing group of speakers are creating their own lingua franca conventions, which are more flexible and fluid than territorial World Englishes (see Seidlhofer 2007).

3.1 English

State borders are generally accepted in English linguistics as playing an important role in shaping linguistic situations. They are an abstraction to a degree and may not the most important level of linguistic variation. Peter Trudgill's classic model of regional and social variation in Britain may serve as a backdrop for visualization (2000, first edition 1974). Figure 3.1 shows the original model by Trudgill for the UK.

Social variation is shown on the vertical axis, geographical variation on the horizontal axis. Standard varieties are found at the top. A pluricentric model starts with the presupposition of, or potential for, several standards of English, which may be translated into several "peaks".

Figure 3.2 adapts Trudgill's model to visualize pluricentric Englishes, in this case for Standard British, Canadian and American English. It shows the three standard varieties as autonomous from each other, with more or less overlap of regional features. Linguistic distance has little bearing in this model. North American features can overlap to a considerable degree with Canadian and Western Canadian features, yet they do not threaten the autonomy of either the Canadian or American standard, as they are conceptualized as different peaks. While Washington State or Oregon English can be rather similar to British Columbia (Canada) English, the model makes clear that American and Canadian forms are heteronomous to—align with—other reference points. Just as the Skåne dialects of Swedish and the Danish dialects near Copenhagen are pictured on theoretical different peaks: they are similar, but no one would attack the autonomy of Swedish by proclaiming, other than in jest, that Skåne Swedish was Danish. It is a matter of respect, actually, *not* to do so. Moreover, Canadian English

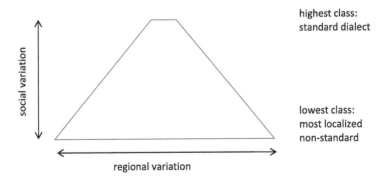

Figure 3.1 Trudgill's model of standard and non-standard dialect

Source: Trudgill (2000: 30)

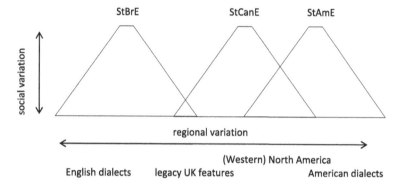

Figure 3.2 Pluricentric depiction of English, with three national standard varieties and feature overlap

overlaps with Standard British English in some registers and uses, but to a lesser degree than it does with American English.

This adaptation allows the modelling of World Englishes in both their standard varieties (the peaks) and regional variations (bottoms), as well as shared and not-shared cross-border features in a surprisingly simple model. The model can incorporate findings from border studies, such as the fact that the "structural distance between the dialects and the standard variety often is not the same across the dialectal territory" (Auer 2011: 492). The argument that some regions in Western Canada and the Western US are similar does not render a pluricentric approach obsolete; on the contrary, the pluricentric approach models such natural behaviour with regional overlap quite elegantly.

3.2 Northern Germanic

The situation in Scandinavia—Denmark, Sweden and Norway—is the prototypical case of *ausbau* languages in which social and political situations have shaped the varieties and our perceptions of them. In order to understand the linguistic developments, one needs to understand the corresponding political and social developments over time. While such historical understanding is necessary in all settings, current social discourse and speaker attitudes always trump any historical connections and disconnections that might exist. What makes the Scandinavian case particularly intriguing is that it clearly demonstrates that without the formation of linguistic centres, in this case in the form of state nations, the three languages would not exist today.

We start the socio-political excursion in the late medieval period. From 1397 to 1523, what is now Denmark, Sweden, Norway and parts of Germany were part of a Danish-led union. Speakers on the ground spoke varieties anywhere on a Northern Germanic dialect continuum, in the south mixing with the Western Germanic varieties and in the north with Finnish, Sami, Russian and the Baltic languages, among others. Until 1814, Norway continued to be in a union with the more powerful Denmark, and from 1814 to 1905 Norway was in a union with the more powerful Sweden, retaining some autonomous status (self-rule). While Norway and the formation of its standard language is the most intriguing part, similar *ausbau* processes affected the development of Standard Danish and Standard Swedish, two standard varieties that retain a very high degree of mutual intelligibility, perhaps more so than an Austrian Styrian speaker's dialect being understood by a speaker of German from Schleswig-Holstein. Until the early 1800s, both Denmark and Sweden retained multilingual empires. In the case of Denmark, the major languages included Danish, Icelandic, German (Schleswig and Holstein) and Faroese. In the case of Sweden, there were above all Swedish, German, Finnish, Estonian and Latvian (Pedersen 2005: 175–176).

The idea of linguistic roofing, introduced at the end of Chapter 2, is vital to understanding the relationships between Danish, Swedish and Norwegian. Was it arbitrary to reshape the Dano-Norwegian, later Swedish-influenced, varieties as Norwegian? Yes, but the *ausbau* character of Norwegian does not invalidate its social importance. Haugen summarizes the codification of Norwegian based on rural dialects that were chosen for their maximal difference from the Danish and Swedish codified forms:

> No single criterion could be found that would at once be universal for Norway and distinctive from her neighbors. The features that were actually widespread in the dialects did not necessarily fit well together into a single linguistic structure [that a standard would be based on, SD].
>
> (Haugen 1966: 300)

Despite this problem, a linguistic structure called Norwegian was created nonetheless. The existence of two written standard varieties that are differentiated in morphology, vocabulary, spelling and to a degree in syntax in Norway is interesting. The two standards, one going back to Ivar Aasen (called Nynorsk, used mostly in rural regions), the other to Knud Knudsen (called Bokmål, associated with the urban centres), have approached one another to a degree, but still represent different varieties (for a concise introduction, see Kerswill 1994: 32–35). This inner-Norwegian variation does not, however, diminish the achievement of the new linguistic centre in Norway with its own "roof". Simplifying greatly, Bokmål (literally "book language") is a variety that is close to the Dano-Norwegian of the upper class Osloers used prior to independence. Bokmål diverts from the Danish standard only in minimal ways, while Nynorsk ("New Norwegian") is a system that codifies maximally different variants that are rooted in western Norwegian rural speech, thus highlighting the differences with Swedish and Danish. While over the twentieth century multiple spelling reforms, above all in 1938 and 1981, have further complicated the relationship of Bokmål and Nynorsk, the fact remains that Bokmål is the dominant system of some 80% of Norwegians, with 20% using Nynorsk (mostly in the west). Today, the two systems are more similar than they used to be, yet both retain language-identificational functions within Norway. Jahr summarizes the later developments: "There are still today two standards for Norwegian, linguistically very close but sociolinguistically clearly different" (2003: 351). The take-home message from the Norwegian case is that without an independent Norwegian state, there would be no Norwegian variety of any kind.

3.3 Belgian Dutch (Flemish) and Dutch Dutch

The situation in Belgian Dutch is defined by a complicated historical relationship between the Flemish (the Belgian Dutch speakers), the Walloons (the Belgian French speakers) and the Dutch speakers in the Netherlands. The relationship has been influenced by political and social developments and is an instructive case of standard reference points, or roofing. Historically, Dutch Dutch has served as a linguistic standard for all Dutch speakers before and since Belgium's foundation as an independent country in 1830. Even today, many Flemish prefer what has been called the "integrationist", i.e. monocentric standard, a standard that is set in the Netherlands and that "integrates" the Dutch-speaking areas by applying the Netherlandic standard to the Flemish regions. As pluricentricity theory predicts, this exonormative relationship is not stable—far from it—and criticism has been mounting for the past 20 to 30 years.

3.3.1 Historical Background

In the Netherlands, the situation at the outset is clear: "the written standard is mirrored in a spoken standard used as the everyday language in a wide variety of contexts by all Dutch" (Grondelaers & van Hout 2011: 209). As a standard variety whose codification was begun after Dutch independence in 1585 (Grondelaers & van Hout 2011: 202–203), standard Dutch Dutch is matched in age and prestige with the other standard languages of Europe. Until the beginning of the twentieth century, regional accents were tolerated and considered part of standard Dutch. It is only after World War II that the prestige factor of the accents of the higher social classes in the Randstad cities (Amsterdam, The Hague, Rotterdam, Utrecht) gained influence.

As a possible reaction to this change, other accents have found more acceptance, so that in present-day spoken Standard Dutch "there is widespread accent variation" (ibid.: 210). New koinés are being created, such as Polder Dutch, which integrates former lower-class pronunciations into standard pronunciations. In other words, diversification as predicted in Schneider's Phase V is alive and well in the Netherlands. Grondelaers and van Hout (2011: 212) draw the provisional conclusion that "identifiable accent variation is a meaningful ingredient of Netherlandic Standard Dutch in the layperson's mind". The evidence points to Dutch Dutch as "demotized", following Mattheier (1997: 7), meaning that the idea of a standard is still undisputed but the standard as such has been relaxed. "Destandardization", in contrast to demotization, questions the very existence of any standard as such.

In Flanders, the Dutch-speaking part of Belgium, standardization was interrupted in the late eighteenth century by foreign rule and was not taken up after 1830, when Belgium became a state. The reason is that in the new state the Walloon French speakers (upper classes) formed the elites, while the Dutch speakers (lower classes) had little control until late in the twentieth century. As a result of the political debate, Flanders took over the Dutch exonormative standard. Dutch was not to be granted official status until 1898 in Belgium (Grondelaers & van Hout 2011: 203), which led to social and functional restrictions in the Flemish varieties. For that reason, the adoption of a fully standardized Dutch, rather than engaging in the process of creating out of the Belgian dialects an endoglossic Belgian Dutch standard, may have been beneficial for the Flemish in the short run:

> After some debate on how this [Belgian Dutch] standard should take shape [. . .] the integrationist ideology gained victory, and the exoglossic Netherlandic Dutch standard (*'Algemeen Beschaafd Nederlands'*) was actively propagated as the language of culture and civilization.
> (Ghyselen, Delarue & Lybaert 2016: 81)

The integrationist victory may have improved the social situation at the time, but "up to this day it continues to determine the language-political agenda in Flanders building on ideologies and discourses that were—and still are—language-political as well as socio-political in nature" (Grondelaers & van Hout 2011: 203).

The above social context is reminiscent of the adoption of the East Central German standard in late eighteenth-century Austria. In Belgium, however, exonormative influence continued in the post-war period. The "Belgian population was actively and consciously encouraged to take over

the Netherlandic standard" (Grondelaers & van Hout 2011: 203), with
TV shows and newspaper columns the Flemish were from the 1950s to
the 1970s taught how to "'clean up' Belgian speech and writing" (ibid.).
Nothing of that kind had occurred in Austria since 1945. On the contrary, a
linguistic self-identity has been fostered, most visibly, perhaps, as of 1951
with the *Österreichisches Wörterbuch* (Austrian dictionary).

Mattheier's concept of demotization is key in both the Flemish and Austrian cases. Once the long process of initial standardization was completed,
as has happened in Europe's bigger languages in the latter half of the nineteenth century, new tensions would arise, stemming from speakers of the
language who had no say in the initial standardization process. Mattheier
(1997: 7) calls this process "extensions in the geographical, social and situational sphere of the standard". Such extensions are not to be understood as
the old standard increasing its sphere but as new standards being created.
Those who were excluded from the formation process faced "special dif-
ficulties with the codified norm" (ibid.), and as a result "a part of the erst-
while dialects and sociolects is being used as a regional and stylistic marker
within the standard". From such marking within a standard, it is only a
small step to the codification of a new standard within a given language.
In the case of Austrian German, that process is considerably advanced (yet
still disputed), while Belgian Dutch is more at its beginning, though with
considerable momentum at present.

3.3.2 Belgian Dutch: Tussentaal, the New Koiné

The past 20 or 30 years have seen interesting developments in Belgian
Dutch. The Dutch used in Flemish Radio and Television (Vlaamse Radio-
en Televisieomroeporganisatie, VRT) is a formal Dutch that some consider
standard. That standard, however, follows the Netherlandic model and is
as a result an ill-suited vehicle to express a Belgian identity. Such identity-
confirming function has been taken over lately by an intermediate variety that developed first in Belgian soap operas and has come to be called
Tussentaal (middle language), as an intermediate super-regional form of
Belgian Dutch that transcends Belgian traditional dialects of Dutch. The
precise character of the variety is still disputed; it is often considered as
"the most controversial spoken variety of present-day Flemish Dutch" and
is described as "a highly vital colloquial variety" in between the standard
and the dialects in Flanders (Grondelaers, van Hout & van Gent 2016:
122). Others point to "inconsistent" perceptual and ideological evidence
about Tussentaal (Ghyselen, Delarue & Lybaert 2016: 81). A third contender for a Belgian standard is the variety of Dutch spoken by Belgian
teachers, "Belgian Teacher Dutch", which might perhaps be paraphrased
as standard Dutch with a Belgian flavour. While accented standard Dutch

is acceptable, perhaps expected, in the Netherlands, such Dutch "is not considered 'beautiful'" in Belgium (Ghyselen, Delarue & Lybaert 2016: 81–82), which seems to be a problem for Belgian Teacher Dutch and would be one reason why it "is not accepted as standard Belgian Dutch (yet)" (ibid.: 82). The Belgian standard situation has been termed a "standard language vacuum" (Grondelaers, van Hout & Speelman, qtd in Ghyselen, Delarue & Lybaert 2016: 82).

As such a vacuum is not good for the linguistic identity of its speakers, it is to be expected that it will be filled before too long. VRT-Dutch does not seem suitable for Flemish linguistic identification. Lybaert (2017) has recently shown that Tussentaal might be undergoing amelioration and is seen less pejoratively than previously, more neutral or even desirable. Vandenbussche summarizes that:

> there is no doubt that (apart from pronunciation) newspapers, radio and television nowadays still recognise the central and guiding role of the Dutch language as used in the north [the Netherlands]. In socio-historical terms one could say that the "integrationist" idea continues to form the basis of the present day language policies in the Flemish media.
> (Vandenbussche 2011: 319)

In other words, if the media is exonormatively confined, linguistic expressions of local and national identities must choose other channels, and in this area, Tussentaal has interesting potential.

There are indeed some indicators that Tussentaal might have the most realistic claim to serve as an identity-confirming variety in the long run, despite current problems of status. Given that the Belgian accents in the standard varieties are not seen as Belgian but rather as tied to the Belgian regions, e.g. Limburg, Brabant, Antwerp (Grondelaers & van Hout 2011: 221), Tussentaal has potential to fill the void. A decade ago, Grondelaers and van Hout concluded that "if there is a standard variety of Belgian Dutch, it is in any case losing ground to the variety of colloquial Belgian Dutch neutrally referred to as *Tussentaal*" (Grondelaers and van Hout 2011: 221), and this development has only accelerated since.

At this point, there is much uncertainty concerning the shaping of Standard Belgian Dutch. In any case, a "clear distinction" should be made "between the language dynamics in the Netherlands and those in Flanders, as the two areas have witnessed very different histories of standardization [. . .], causing very diverging conditions in which current standard language change processes are operating" (Ghyselen, Delarue & Lybaert 2016: 79). Such separation can directly be transferred to the context of Austria and Bavaria. If one equates the two situations, one will fail to see important differences.

3.3.3 Destandardization, Demotization and the Notion of "Standard"

Two terms have frequently been used to characterize changes in European standard varieties in the past two or three generations. First, there is Mattheier's demotization, as introduced above. It refers to a process of language change in which the concept of a standard ideology stays intact, yet what is considered standard is widened i.e. more informal ways of speaking find acceptance into the standard. Second, the concept of destandardization describes a process in which the established standard language loses its position as the best variety, which eventually leads to an abandonment of the standard-language ideology (Coupland & Kristiansen 2011: 28). In practical terms, it will be difficult to tell demotization from destandardization, which can only succeed with access to language attitudinal and language perceptual speaker data.

In the Dutch context, identity formations seem to play an important role, with different groups expressing different preferences, such as in the case of Poldernederlands, for which "speaker evaluation experiments have shown that young Dutch women subconsciously evaluate Poldernederlands more positively than older Dutch women" (Ghyselen, Delarue & Lybaert 2016: 78). Recent attitude studies position Tussentaal as a kind of unmarked colloquial variety in everyday non-local conversations in which dialects would have been used until recently:

> dialect is for example described as broad on the one hand, and cozy and juicy on the other hand, and Standard Dutch evokes characterisations as beautiful or as decent, polished and civilized, but also as stiff and dull. In comparison, tussentaal appears to be less marked to our respondents. [. . .] To most of our respondents tussentaal appears to be the unmarked middle-ground between two marked poles.
>
> (Lybaert 2017: 113)

This characterization is not dissimilar from the German concept of Umgangssprache, or the colloquial standard, and from that data it seems that Tussentaal is the best candidate for a Standard Belgian Dutch at present.

3.4 Luxembourgish

Not all situations are as complex as the Belgian standard of Dutch. By contrast, Luxembourg is a picture-book example of how a dialect of language X (German) can become language Y (Luxembourgish) in a very short time, that is, in less than three generations. Historically, Luxembourgish is a dialect of Western Moselle German, and within Luxemburg four traditional dialect regions can be found, which is significant as internal variation is often taken as a counter argument against pluricentric approaches in German. Until 1839, Luxembourg was attached to other states—the Spanish, the Austrians and the French—so that, like Belgium, its initial formation happened quite late. With statehood, Luxembourgish underwent a first gain in prestige, which only after WWII considerably increased (Gilles 2000: 200).

The linguistic situation has usually been described as triglossic: Luxembourgish (Lëtzebuergesch), French and German. While traditionally, French and German dominated in the written medium, the spoken realm was the domain of Luxembourgish. An "increasing use of French as a spoken language coupled with the more frequent appearance of Luxembourgish as a written language" (Horner 2005: 166) has changed the original distribution. While the increase of Luxembourgish has had a motivation in the increase of sociolinguistic distance to German after World War II, the biggest increases in use are linked with the arrival of EU institutions, the opening of the banking sector and immigration. With Luxembourgers in the minority in their own country (just about one in three residents holds a Luxembourg passport), it seems clear that language was adapted as a vehicle to express cultural identity to a greater degree than before the massive opening of the country to investments. The 1984 language law was a key moment in the adoption and codification of Luxembourgish, as "this law is connected to the perceived need for a legitimate national language to justify the continued existence of an autonomous nation-state as well as of Luxembourgish identity" (Horner 2005: 169).

Luxembourgish was codified into a language of its own only after World War II, though discussions about its elaboration into a standard language go back to at least 1855 (Gilles 2000: 202). These predecessor stages were important in that they were rooted in the spoken language. The writing system was at the time the German one, which did not lend itself to establishing a national written language. Gilles (2000: 207–209) suggests that the concept of a negatively defined oral koiné was instrumental in conceptualizations of spoken Luxembourgish in an effort to "unite" the four dialect regions in a non-identifiable, "balanced" koiné that includes features of all. Gilles argues that a koiné did not exist by then, but as linguists took over this interpretation "uncritically" (ibid.: 207), it put the koiné conceptually as an over-arching entity and umbrella term above the traditional dialects, which led to the construction of the standard variety. As all standard varieties are constructed, the process of "uncritically" taking on the historical koiné-interpretation expedited the codification of Luxembourgish. In locations where linguists do chime in, as in the case of Belgian Dutch or Austrian German, the *ausbau* varieties are generally delayed. This begs the question to what degree linguists who abide by the rule not to interfere with language planning issues do so anyway simply by virtue of taking a more conservative position.

Big strides have been made since World War II, with efforts to regularize orthography as early as 1946. Since the 1984 language legislation, Luxembourgish has made great progress towards a fully fledged national language. Luxembourgish is "regarded by the speech community as a language of its own. As a consequence, German is considered a different language"(Gilles & Trouvain 2013: 67) today. Not just in the longer historical context, Luxembourgish is a good example of an *ausbau* language, changing its status via its functions and only to a small degree its linguistic forms. Claiming that Luxembourgish was German would be inevitably perceived as negating the existence of the Grand Duchy of Luxembourg, as it is "the first language of most Luxembourgers [and] also has the status of the national language (since 1984)" (ibid.).

As of late, computer-mediated communication has helped establish the language further in the written medium. As Belling and de Bres (2014) have shown in their experiment of a user-led Facebook group to "get and donate things for free", Luxembourgish is the overwhelmingly used language in the group, though initially other languages dominated and only with time, through linguistic negotiations, language use and acts of identity expression, did Luxembourgish come to dominate. From the initial 0% of posts in Luxembourgish (and 100% in English, with a tiny fraction of English–Luxembourgish code-switching), after successive increases over time, a surprising 88% of all postings (n = 337) (Belling & de Bres 2014: Figure 3.2) were written in Luxembourgish. The authors summarize:

> In the end Luxembourgish dramatically trumped the more established languages of written communication in Luxembourg—French and German—in this context, as well as taking over from English. For a language still classified by UNESCO as "vulnerable", Luxembourgish experiences a high degree of vitality in this group.
>
> (Belling & de Bres 2014: 85)

The study is evidence of the momentum of Luxembourgish as a language of choice, expressing identity formations, rather than a language that was politically mandated—first in opposition to German, then to reaffirm one's identity in the international and EU contexts. I argue in this book that the continued codification of Austrian German would have a similarly liberating effect that all German speakers, not just Austrians, would benefit from.

4 The German "Pluri-Areal" Model

In light of the evidence from other languages and contexts, one might wonder how German standard varieties could be modelled differently. This is particularly so as the pluricentric perspective has been studied for German in detail in Ammon et al.'s *Variantenwörterbuch* (2004, 2016) and is accessible in Kellermeier-Rehbein's (2014) textbook and Schmidlin's (2011) attitude study, as well as in Pfrehm's (2007) dissertation. Major proponents of German dialectology, however, offer statements that are in clear contradiction of basic pluricentric principles.

While the arguments that are brought forth against pluricentricity will be dealt with in detail one by one, it is worthwhile to highlight the main objection up front. "Pluri-arealists" operate with strict cut-off points. The main point is that both Austrian and Swiss Standard German are alleged not to be "different enough" to constitute varieties national. While the "enough" is never defined, a big deal is made of not being different enough, as in the case to Austrian German:

> One can argue that less than two per cent of variation in standard German lexis and pronunciation and even less variation in grammar does hardly make a "variety".
>
> (Elspaß & Niehaus 2014: 50)

That argument finds further expression in the call for absolute, neat-and-tidy variants that are confined exclusively to non-dominant varieties. It is claimed that such absolute variants are in the minority:

> Only in a minority of cases [do] variants occur specifically only in one country in absolute frequency. Most variants are rather non-specific, i.e. they also occur in other countries and regions, but are "not common core German, which means that they are not used in all German-speaking areas" (Ammon et al. 2016: XVIII). In the majority of cases,

there is a side-by-side of "relative variants", i.e. no single variant is used exclusively (with "absolute" frequency).

(Elspaß, Dürscheid & Ziegler 2017: 73)

The demand for categorical variables (for which the term "absolute frequency" is used) is an excessive criterion, given that we are dealing with varieties of mutual intelligibility. On a more abstract level, one would argue that under such a criterion, not a single language or variety would have been able to develop, as language does not work with categorical but with degrees of differences, likelihoods and proportional categories.

An unrealistic requirement of categoricity lies at the heart of the "pluri-arealist's" objection, which can be shown below in one of Scheuringer's statements, where he questions and somewhat undermines the basis of World Englishes. The ad-hoc word creations and puns are quite typical in this writing:

Is pluricentric, the way it is now understood, not actually "pluri-un-centric", or even "pluri-centralist"? Entire countries as centres? *One* centre from Kiel [in the utmost north in Germany] to Berchtesgaden [in the very south]? I doubt that the term reflects the situation in Anglophone countries and I object that it reflects the situation in the German-speaking countries.

(Scheuringer 1997: 343)

It is this idea of categoricity that is, by virtue of defending a status quo, selectively applied to non-dominant varieties. When ECG was set as the standard, for instance, it did not include categorical rule requirements. That the argument is indefensible can be seen from the thought experiment that, by that logic, if only one German German speaker uses Austrian or Swiss variants, it undermines the legitimacy of Standard Austrian and Standard Swiss German. The treatment of pluricentricity as an unjustified abstraction is rooted in a de-historical rhetoric that has a pluri-areal standard de facto enshrined as the German German standard and as the standard for all German-speaking areas.

Meanwhile, graduate student work has come forth in this line of thought. Sutter, for instance, summarizes the representation of regional variation in German dictionaries in a pluri-areal light, claiming while German dictionaries adhere to a pluricentric model, they do so because it is easier to do. This, she writes, is understandable given the complexities of the data collection:

A reason [for the preference of pluricentricity in German dictionaries] is surely the lesser complexity of the pluricentric model, because in the

pluri-areal model the German-speaking areas are divided into regions
that are based on dialectal zones. These regions cannot be clearly separated from one another, because they do not rely on an extralinguistic
criterion (national border).

(Sutter 2017: 273)

What is left unreflected in Sutter's argument is that the dialect zones did
not arrive out of nowhere, solely based on linguistic data. That Austria,
for instance, is represented by four dialect zones in the pluri-areal roster
of regions is not a given, nor is the division of the German-speaking area
into 15 zones (e.g. Niehaus 2017). In this context, the four Austrian dialect
zones are essentialized at the expense of other configurations, such as a
national Austrian level. "Pluri-areality" is incompatible with pluricentric
theory. As we have seen, Scheuringer goes so far as to doubt the approach
taken in English linguistics, rather than questioning his own stance, which
he has been repeating since Scheuringer (1990b) and, as will be shown, in
an unexplained contradiction to Scheuringer (1985).

4.1 Dialectological Context

In traditional European dialectology, it is customary to think that a political border cutting across traditional dialect zones "has had little impact on
pre-existing dialect continua" (Woolhiser 2011: 501). This view has been
changing since Kremer's (1979) pioneering work on the German–Dutch
border. In this way, the German–Dutch border is well studied (e.g. contributions in Kremer 1993, such as Hinskens 1993, or Lenz, Gooskens & Reker
2009).

It seems as though many, mostly smaller European countries show a
desire for new national standard varieties and even entirely new standard
languages. As we saw in Chapter 2, Luxembourg and its codification of
Luxembourgish is such an example. Gilles (1999) has shown that "the
[Luxembourg] dialects in the eastern border regions are becoming less like
those of neighbouring parts of Belgium['s German-speaking areas] and
Germany" (qtd. in Woolhiser 2011: 508). It is the effect of what Auer (2011:
497) summarizes succinctly: "former common standards dissolve by repertoire splits (Belgium/Netherlands, Austria/Germany, Croatia/Serbia etc.)"
into new endoglossic standards. We can see that standard languages are
malleable and responsive to social changes, which fits well with the social
definition of a language and the impossibility of defining it on exclusively
linguistic grounds.

In recent European history, there has also been the reverse case of separation as in the Czech/Slovak case. This scenario is the merger of two
separate states, merging a geographical dialect continuum that was split for

four decades by an impermeable border. This case is the (capitalist) Federal Republic of Germany (FRG) and the (communist) German Democratic Republic (GDR), the latter of which was integrated into the Federal Republic in 1990. While in West Berlin urban vernacular Berlinish was stigmatized, in East Berlin—which was the capital of the GDR—that citylect had developed into an "urban colloquial variety", a variety that had begun to spread beyond the city limits (Woolhiser 2011: 509). This is precisely as pluricentricity theory predicts, based on principles of socioeconomic prestige and the interplay with standard varieties. That the GDR standard was not very different from the FRG variety is owed to the relatively short time of the GDR's existence. One can see, however, that a short separation of four decades or two generations (of an admittedly very brutal kind) can produce supraregional norms that, eventually, would be codified into a new standard. The GDR had its own Duden dictionary (based in Leipzig), while the FRG had a rival operation in Mannheim. German Unification put an end to the pluricentristically predictable development.

At this point, major proponents of pluri-areality object. Elspaß and Niehaus (2014) demonstrate a misunderstanding of the idea of roofing and national variety in the case of the GDR/FRG standard:

> Firstly, it [pluricentricity] is an entirely political concept, based on the notion of *Überdachung* [roofing] of the language area by a political state. As for the recent history of German, this would have had the somewhat odd consequence that on 3 October 1990, the German language has lost [sic] an entire national variety, namely GDR German, literally overnight. Secondly, from a linguistic perspective, one may ask whether "national varieties of German" are really varieties?
>
> (Elspaß & Niehaus 2014: 50)

The above quote rejects the social and political dimension of language, as if language, especially its standard varieties, could be treated in a social vacuum. Is there a political dimension to standard varieties? Yes, there is, and it captures, for instance, the difference between Bavaria (part of Germany) and Austria (an independent nation): while Austria has a claim to a national variety, Bavaria, starting from a similar linguistic base, does not. While Bavaria joined the German Empire, Austria was pushed out by Prussia. Standard Austrian German is a late consequence of the "kleindeutsch solution" (Germany without Austria).

4.2 Pluricentric and Monocentric Models of German

German has been linguistically conceptualized as a pluricentric language since the late 1940s, when the new Austrian government issued an Austrian dictionary for use in government and schools. First published in 1951, the *Österreichisches Wörterbuch* started a discourse around the various forms of national standards (for Austria, e.g. Moosmüller 1991; Moosmüller, Schmid & Brandstätter 2015; de Cillia 1998). Figure 4.1 shows three national standard varieties of German—Standard German German, Standard Austrian German and Standard Swiss German—in line with Clyne (1995) and in analogy to Figure 3.2 for English.

The model depicts shared, cross-border features and regional features on the non-standard level between Swiss dialects and the Austrian province of Vorarlberg (the only sizeable non-Bavarian–Austrian dialect region in Austria) and, most relevant for the present chapter, the Upper Austrian and German dialects in Bavaria. Both Upper Austrian and Bavarian dialects historically derive from the same dialect region, i.e. the "Bavarian–Austrian" dialects.

The situation in Switzerland is comparable to Austria. While Swiss dialects are used as identity markers, the Swiss standard variety is distinctly recognizable. While a diglossic model with high variety—standard—and low variety—dialects—captures the situation more clearly in Switzerland than in Austria, where a diaglossic situation with a less clear cut-off between the variants is seen, the basic bi-dialectal situation is equivalent. For Standard Swiss German, "the concept of national variety [. . .] and with it the pluricentric approach applies best" (Schmidlin 2017: 100).

Recent years have seen the pluri-areal paradigm expanding in German linguistics at the expanse of the pluricentric approach. Pluri-areal says nothing more than that the German language is subject to regional (geographical) variation, which extends across national boundaries. It implies, since it was coined as an alternative construct to pluricentricity, that there are no standard varieties of German other than the traditional one, which is based

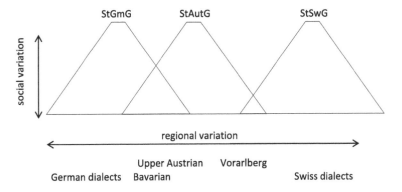

Figure 4.1 Pluricentric conceptualization of German

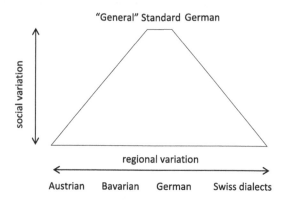

Figure 4.2 Implicit model of standard and dialects in "pluri-areality": the ONE STANDARD GERMAN AXIOM

on East Central German as a result of Gottsched's and Adelung's popularity. Proponents of "pluri-areality" are proponents of a monocentric approach to Standard German, as shown in Figure 4.2.

In English, such monocentric views would need to be called colonial: the bigger, more powerful nation gets to set the standard for the smaller, independent one. In the German context, I call this concept the ONE STANDARD GERMAN AXIOM, which underpins the pluri-areal line of thought. Findings from the Canada–US border, for instance, are of direct relevance to the situation in Austria and Germany (e.g. Avis 1954, 1955, 1956; Boberg 2000; Chambers 1998; 2008; Dollinger 2012a; Dollinger & Clarke 2012; Dollinger & Fee 2017; Dollinger 2019a; Labov, Ash & Boberg 2005). As will be shown throughout this book, a profoundly monocentric mindset underpins the pluri-areal approach in contradiction to its goal stating the opposite, which is to reject an "idealized standard notion" (Elspaß, Dürscheid & Ziegler 2017: 71). This rejection of an "idealized standard", however, falls short as it does not consider the codified standard but only its implementation ("Gebrauchsstandard") in a framework that claims not to rely on a monocentric German German ideology ("monozentrischen 'Binnendeutsch' Ideologie") (ibid.). As Chapters 5 and 6 will demonstrate, a monocentric bias is, despite the set goals, the inevitable outcome of the methodological design and atheoretical stance of pluri-areal work.

4.3 The Upper Austrian–Bavarian Border

The Austrian–Bavarian border is an especially interesting situation. The border region entails the *Innviertel*, which is one of four parts of the province of Upper

Austria that used to belong to Bavaria until 1779. After some back and forth until 1816, the Innviertel was finally ceded to Austria. Braunau on the Inn is the Austrian town on the right bank of the Inn River; Simbach, its German neighbour in Bavaria on the river's left bank, is connected by a bridge (Figure 4.4). From Braunau, about 60 km downstream to Passau, where the Inn merges with the Danube (Figure 4.3), the river is the international border between the Innviertel south and east of the river and Bavaria to the north and west.

Figure 4.4 shows the Inn bridge at Braunau (in the front) and Simbach (beyond the river), with the border booth depicted in the background. The booth was used until the start of the EU Schengen joint border regime in 1999 for border checks and customs. As a result of the migrant refugee crisis, it has been used sporadically again since September 2015.

The Inn River is a realistic barrier that prevents the integration of the relatively small towns on each side of the river. While seven relevant border crossings are located between Salzburg City and Passau (see Figure 4.3), in addition to a highway crossing that is mostly used for long-distance travel, the border is a social and cognitive boundary of significance.

Crossing is possible in or near Wals (land crossing), Freilassing (land), Laufen (bridge), Burghausen (bridge), Braunau (bridge), Obernberg (bridge) and Passau (bridge). Despite the bridges, the border is a cognitive

Figure 4.3 Upper Austrian (and Salzburg) and Bavarian border region

Figure 4.4 Bridge over the Inn River at Braunau (front) and Simbach
Source: Wikimedia Commons. Photo: Mattes, CC BY-SA 3.0

"boundary" that is not crossed without a reason. The context of Braunau/ Simbach is comparable to the cross-border settings in New Brunswick, Canada and Maine, USA, though the North American towns, also separated by a bridge, do share services such as a fire department and a movie theatre, which is not the case in this example.

On that border, Burnett (2006) shows a Canadian English influence on US English in the North American setting, and not the other way around, in an important reminder that not all influence extends from the larger to the smaller country. As in the context of St. Stephen, New Brunswick and Calais, Maine, the Canadian town is the bigger one, just as Braunau in Austria is with 16,000 inhabitants bigger than Simbach with 9,000. With the exception of Passau (50,000), these two cities are by far the biggest ones along the border north of Salzburg until the Inn meets the Danube in an essentially rural space.

4.4 A Pluricentrist Turned Pluri-Arealist

Braunau/Simbach is the locus of creation of pluri-areality. Scheuringer (1990a) is the first and so far *only* study of cross-border fieldwork in Braunau and Simbach. While the term pluri-areal is not yet used in that study, its data interpretation is directly responsible for the term's popularization. Scheuringer (1990a) is a qualitative work. Given the complex patterns at hand that require quantification, qualitative studies are exposed to bias in the absence of adequate theoretical safeguards. The effects of Scheuringer's study go "far beyond the particular context" (Dollinger 2016a) in its attack on pluricentricity, which warrants a close look in the present context.

It is news today that Scheuringer initially worked in a pluricentric framework. In a paper apparently unknown in German linguistic circles, he (1985: 447) speaks of the "linguistic re-orientation" and *"Austrianization* of the Innviertel" as a result of the 1816 border realignment. We also read there, clearly in line with the pluricentric model, the following:

> Irrespective of the "comparative uniformity of Bavarian as a whole" (Noble 1983:76), characteristic features have developed on either side of the [Upper Austrian–Bavarian] border. [. . .] Being a nation with a long tradition of statehood, Austria has developed a specific variety of German in the same way as English shows different varieties in different parts of the world. There has never been sufficient reason to postulate an Austrian language, of course, although now and then aspirations arose for some sort of linguistic demarcation towards Germany. [. . .] On the whole, the concept of an Austrian variety of standard German is generally accepted (for Austrian German cf. Reifenstein 1973 and Wiesinger 1983).
>
> (Scheuringer 1985: 447, English original)

Within five years, Scheuringer was to perform an intellectual U-turn. There is nothing special about changing one's stance, as long as such changes are rationalized as a vital part of the knowledge creation process. What makes Scheuringer's case special is that the reversal was carried out without documented reasoning. A change of such magnitude, arguing against a Standard Austrian German and adopting the ONE STANDARD GERMAN AXIOM, would call for extensive commentary.

Scheuringer's study presents select findings from four locations each in Upper Austria and Bavaria. It exclusively focuses on the traditional dialects around Braunau and Simbach and not on standard varieties. The raw data are generally not presented so that only verbal qualitative summaries are offered. Rejecting pluricentricity, Scheuringer concludes his study, saying that there

> are summarily only minor differences between the Bavarian and the Austrian areas [. . .], which are for the biggest part differences which are best interpreted as developments that have taken place since the separation into two states.
>
> (Scheuringer 1990a: 424)

This assessment is conducted without a yardstick of what is "major" and not. Throughout the book, the reader sees in the little raw data that is offered the equivalent of what can be considered clear patterns of pluricentricity.

We are informed, for instance, that vocabulary is "explicable on account of the different countries und practically always derive from the standard language and the higher social non-standard varieties" (Scheuringer 1990a: 404). However, this finding has no bearing on the overall interpretation that the cross-border differences are "minor".

The limited raw data is most interesting, however. Figure 4.5 shows two variables from Scheuringer's cross-border data. On the left is the sequence of (what used to be) Middle High German (MHG.) -*il*-, as in *Milch* ("milk") or *Hilfe* ("help"), which is vocalized in a number of ways. South of the black line is Upper Austrian Braunau; to the north is Bavarian Simbach. Clear diversion and conversion patterns emerge, in line with pluricentric theory. In three of the four Austrian locations, a vocalization in -*ui*- is realized. Both are different from the majority Bavarian -*ei*- with one case of (predominantly Austrian) -*ui*-. This is a clear border effect of what once was the same dialect zone; it is, as predicted by pluricentric theory and the effect of roofing, influenced by gravity theory (Trudgill 1974; Boberg 2000), in which the bigger town (Braunau), using -*ui*-, would influence the smaller German in Simbach, with -*ei*-, were it not for the border. This finding is also fully in line with Burnett's (2006) Canada–US findings.

It is a similar picture on the right, for MHG. -*el*- in Germany is -*ei*-, i.e. *kalben* is *keiben*, *Schale* is *Schei*, *stellen* is *steien* in all four locations. Whereas on the Austrian side we have *koiben*, *Schoin*, *stoin*, with one

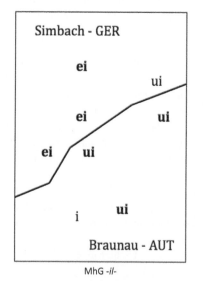
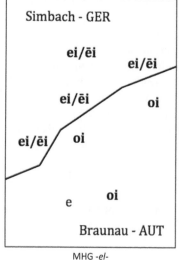

Figure 4.5 Cross-border dialect data from Scheuringer

Source: Scheuringer (1990a: maps 10 & 11)

monophthongal variant *-e-*, so *kehben, Schehle, stehn*. This distribution is, again, different from the Bavarian ones.

Such distributions instil doubt in the validity of Scheuringer's overall interpretations. Critical voices were indeed present from early on. Ludwig Zehetner's review is quite clear in its overall assessment, when he says, contrary to the study's conclusion, that

> most of the differences in the regions of Braunau and Simbach are to be deemed the results of the border realignment of 1779.
>
> (Zehetner 1995: 355)

The most interesting part of the data seems to have been missed, while trying not to part with the ONE STANDARD GERMAN AXIOM that Scheuringer adopted at some point between 1985 and 1990. Wiesinger sees the case somewhat similarly in his discussion of research perspectives, referring to "Scheuringer and Pohl [as] trivializing the Austrian features in favour of the shared features with Old Bavaria and more generally the Upper German dialect zone" (Wiesinger 2000: 556). Heinz-Dieter Pohl has since modified his position and clearly recognizes Austrian features and Austrian identity today as expressed in Standard Austrian German, while not neglecting features that are shared with Germany (cp. Pohl 1997, 2017).

It is clear that Scheuringer takes exception to linguistic variety planning "by indiscriminately transferring eastern Austrian and especially Viennese linguistic facts to all of Austria" (1990a.: 407). In particular, he takes exception to Viennese influence in western Austria. The frequent use of ad-hoc terms in Scheuringer (1990a) muddy the waters unnecessarily. For instance, where once *Kren* ("horse-radish") was used on both sides of the border, in Bavaria, the older *Kren* was ousted by Standard German German *Meerrettich*. This effect, which we know as linguistic autonomy (Chambers & Trudgill 1998) or roofing (Kloss 1978), is confusingly called "pressure on the dialect" ("Dialektalitätsdruck"). It is unclear why no theory was applied, or even basic principles such as Occam's razor. If we applied Occam's razor, a principle stating that the theory requiring the fewest presuppositions is preferred, to Scheuringer's data, we would have a picture-book cross-border case for pluricentricity.

It is obvious in the scholarly perception of the Austrian–German border that effects that are the result of the younger national border seem to be trivialized. This is because Scheuringer's study was the first to adopt implicitly the idea of "pluri-areality" and must have met a need for the "post-national" reasoning so common, as Whaley (2002) has shown, in much of German humanistic writing. I argue that this development has considerably clouded the discussion. Scheuringer (1990a) presents no data with which he could meaningfully speak to standard varieties, other than the role that traditional dialects may play in the formation of a standard. That role is limited to the feeding in of select dialectal features in the formation of a new standard (Auer 2005: 28), though dialectal cross-differences are by no means a requirement.

The objection that traditional dialects have no bearing on the standard is therefore not correct. As both Bavaria and Upper Austria belong to the Middle Bavarian dialect zone, the pluricentric perspective offers in the form of a standard a higher layer, on top of older substrates, that is not totally independent from the dialects that are spoken on the ground (as depicted in Figure 4.1). Different linguistic features are combined to feed into the sociolinguistic relevance of political borders and

> divergence [across the border] can be expected to increase to the degree that (in this order) (a) the national standard languages, (b) the repertoire types (diaglossic/diglossic), or (c) the regional dialects differ on both sides of the border.
>
> (Auer 2005: 28)

In other words, when the dialects along the border diversify, as Scheuringer (1990a) shows, such diversification is expected to have a modest positive effect towards the formation and acceptance of a new standard variety. Such reasoning, though, is replaced by near-programmatic statements, such as the following extreme stance:

> All in all one issue seems to be clear: It would be presumptuous, given the historical–cultural connections between Bavaria and Austria, to postulate a linguistic boundary. In the face of an internal dialectal delimitation of the Austrian–Bavarian dialects that was set almost a millennium ago, the [current] border, finalized in its present form as late as 1816, is a recent divide of lesser significance. The question of significance poses itself, however, in the form of a border between strictly regional varieties of a language and here, in particular, in reference to an overarching German dialect that is used in two countries.
>
> (Scheuringer 1990b: 372)

Scheuringer's study is pre-Labovian in that it employs qualitative assessments of field data. We have no idea how many tokens of a particular variant, in a given setting and on what occasion were analysed; we also have no idea about speech styles elicited, a crucial aspect of Labovian sociolinguistics, and we have no way to replicate the findings, as the data is not reported.

Postulations as the one above are not helpful. Neither is Scheuringer's dictum that (1996: 151) "Deutsch ist eine pluriareale Sprache" (German is a pluri-areal language), as it says nothing more than "German is a language that varies geographically". Since there is no language that does not have that feature, our knowledge gain is indeed nil. As a new term has been introduced that does not add any theoretical or descriptive substance, it clouds the picture in opposition to pluricentricity. "Pluri-areality" is a step backwards from a pluricentric approach and its commitment to explicit theory testing.

Many years ago, Scheuringer (1985) offered a convincingly argued and avant-garde-like paper at the time on pluricentricity, as the following passage illustrates (in open contrast to Scheuringer 1990a up to the present, see 2017):

> German dialectology has not yet [in 1985] achieved a balanced consideration of theoretical as well as practical aspects, and pragmatics is sometimes still confused with vague intuition. In the face of a wealth of theoretical and practical data the synthesis is to be accomplished soon; the path to "Labovian deal" has been laid.
>
> (Scheuringer 1985: 444)

Addressing its isolationism, one of the problems in German dialectology, the announcement is not enacted in Scheuringer (1990a), which is already in opposition to pluricentricity, thereby negating the existence of Standard Austrian German.

5 The Case Against Pluricentricity

Austria and Germany have a difficult history. So much so that in the wake of these sister countries' conflicts, and other factors, the world was implicated into two world wars. There are a number of scenarios of how the countries' relationship may have been shaped differently. Had Austria and Germany become one country, as seemed likely until about 1850, it would have been under Austrian leadership in the Holy Roman Empire of the German Nation. Alternatively, if at the end of World War I the much smaller German-speaking parts of Austria had been allowed, as their population majorities originally wished, to join Germany, we would be dealing with utterly different sociolinguistic problems in the smaller German-speaking countries. Austria would then be another Bavaria, which, though powerful and large, would have relinquished its independence for German Unification under Prussian leadership in 1871. But that did not happen.

5.1 Pluricentricity and the *Österreichisches Wörterbuch* (ÖWB)

After 1945, Austria managed to establish an independent nation within 20 years that, in explicit contrast to Germany, was trying to connect to its imperial legacy in its new form of a dwarf state. While approval ratings for an "Austrian nation" were still modest in the 1950s, they began a steep upwards climb in the 1960s. In the early 1990s, four in five Austrians considered their country a nation in its own right (Wiesinger 2000: 556).

There were early attempts to give linguistic expression to a new Austrian identity. The publication of the *Österreichisches Wörterbuch* (ÖWB) in 1951, in opposition to the Duden dictionaries, the leading German dictionaries since 1906, was a courageous sociolinguistic–political project. The step towards the ÖWB was remarkable as it happened very early, coinciding with the first scholarly collection of World Englishes (Partridge & Clark 1951).

The reception of ÖWB has initially been quite negative, especially among the Austrian elites, which included many German philologists who loathed it. According to Krassnig (1958: 156), who carried out the bulk of the work for the first edition of 1951 (Wiesinger 2006: 179), the ÖWB was labelled a "superfluous, sign-of-the times, offensive" project that was geared against "Gesamtdeutschtum", which may be translated as "common Germanness", or Großdeutschtum. Such negative reaction against a dictionary aiming to document Austrian German rather than German German is in itself an indicator of social and identificational uncertainty: for some reason, Austrian German should not be allowed to exist, in the opinion of some *großdeutsch*-thinking minds. In the 1950s, those who were still dreaming of a united Germany—Großdeutschland—despite the Nazi Anschluss and catastrophe between 1938 and 1945, still held some sway. The role of the ÖWB, however, was cemented despite fierce opposition with the schoolbook program, which benefitted all students in Austria. Since the start of the program in the mid-1970s, every student has received schoolbooks up to grade 9 for free, which includes a free copy of the ÖWB.

The ÖWB is remarkable and internationally quite unrivalled for its role as a dictionary socialization tool in Austria. After an initial print of 20,000 in 1951, by June 1954 a total of 173,000 copies had been sold and 20 years later, in May 1973, a total of 1,767,000 (ÖWB 32nd edition, 1973: inner cover verso). Today, after 44 years of the free schoolbook campaign in Austria, this official dictionary, as adopted by the Austrian Ministry of Education in 1968, has seen a circulation in the range 5 to 6 million copies, which is unparalleled with any other dictionary in Austria. Because the goals and claims of the 42nd edition from 2012 are noticeably muted, the 32nd edition gives a better characterization of the aspirations of the work, which includes the documentation of the Austrian colloquial standard (Umgangssprache) and dialect words, which have been rendered in standardized spellings. It bills itself as a dictionary in opposition to the East Central German standard when it proclaims in the preface:

> We Austrians use an array of expressions, which are no less correct, no worse nor less beautiful than those used elsewhere. They were naturally preferably entered into the dictionary, while those that are used for instance only in Northern Germany are not considered at all or, if entered, they are marked as foreign or at least unusual.
>
> (ÖWB-32, 1973: 6)

The above is a balanced statement in favour of linguistic autonomy while at the same time seeking to maintain a Common Core German. The ÖWB is the most widely used dictionary in Austria and, with the help of the schoolbook program, probably the most frequently sold book in the country.

5.2 The Charge of Ideology vs. Enregistering Identity

The mid-1990s saw a vigorous debate between proponents of the pluricentricity and pluri-areality. The most heated exchange was Muhr (1996) and Scheuringer (1996), featuring two Austrian linguists working from different assumptions. Muhr, who has made substantial contributions on Austrian German since the early 1980s, on the one hand, subscribes to a pluricentric model:

> The only option is a functional approach, which assumes the language of a given country as a given and considers its description and particular use as legitimate, without severing any ties beyond one's state borders. There is no reason to consider one's own German as "worse" than any other variety that comes from abroad or to link a focus on one's own linguistic idiosyncrasies with nationalist tendencies.
>
> (Muhr 1996: 15)

Muhr's words seem in line with the international model. Scheuringer, however rejects such model categorically in an "anti-national stance", because

> state nations or nations defined through language and nationalisms have, in my opinion, until today caused so many catastrophes in Europe that these notions are unsuited as concepts in the long term.
>
> (Scheuringer 1996: 151)

The provoking undertones are obvious in the above quote—who would want to agree that nationalism was a good development in the first half of the twentieth century?—yet there is no factual argument presented. Scheuringer rejects a possible national component as a theoretical concept because of the atrocities in twentieth-century Europe that were conducted in the name of nationalism. One is reminded of what McColl Millar's (2005: 9) calls "the mid-twentieth century distrust of nationalism" in the light of two world wars. As I have pointed out above, this is not the kind of nationalism that is expressed in concepts such as Standard Austrian German, where the goal is an affirmation of identities.

Scheuringer's reasoning, while understandable, does of course not per se render "nation" invalid as an independent linguistic variable. The argument, however, is poised to avoid a debate about the more positive aspects of nationalism as an identity-confirming rather than a destructive notion. This notion is of great relevance to many speakers: the vindication of their German as a legitimate standard, or if not their German, then at least the German they hear from their news anchors, radio and TV personalities, such as Armin Wolf, Susanne Höggerl, Rainer Hazviar or Nadja Bernhard and *not* that of Anne Will, Günther Jauch, Marietta Slomka or Jörg Pilawa, though the latter are brilliant in their domain.

The unease with nationalism has left its mark on work on Austrian German. In Einar Haugen's classic study of the codification of Norwegian, we can find a solution to the problem. As if replying to Scheuringer's statement, Haugen wrote in the 1960s:

> Such negative judgements [of nationalism] are understandable in the light of world events. But they need to be tempered by an insight into the positive sides of nationalism. As was noted earlier . . . nationalism wears two faces: an external image which must be sufficiently distinctive to be identified by outsiders, and an internal image which overrides local loyalties and permits all citizens to identify themselves with it. Nationalism is not only or even primarily directed against outsiders; it is also a sentiment of cohesion among the members of the nation, a loyalty which transcends the parochial or regional attachments of the primitive community.
>
> (Haugen 1966: 278)

The charge of ideological–political motivations behind a pluricentric model is habitually heard in the pluri-areal camp. We have seen that Elspaß and Niehaus (2014: 50) consider national varieties "an entirely political concept", thereby neglecting the linguistic realities that speakers of non-dominant varieties find themselves in. Such realities include the fact that today, in democratic societies, linguistic norms—the majority use—should find uptake in the linguistic codices. Today, model speakers, educated model speakers who were socialized in Austria, must be given precedence in a codification of Standard Austrian German (Muhr's 2007 pronunciation dictionary seeks to do just that).

Franz Grillparzer was aware of the issue in the 1860s; Anglicist Karl Luick codified Austrian idiosyncrasies in the standard around 1900; and Ludwig Wittgenstein actively promoted Austrian German in the 1920s. Today, in a hopefully soon to be integrated Europe, where symbolic means of identification become more and more important, national standard varieties are an effective means of linguistic identification beyond the regional level. If someone travels within the EU or beyond, what people usually remember first about someone is their nationality: "Ah, the *Austrian*". Later, people will discover more nuanced shades of identity, the *linguist*, the one playing the guitar or the like.

Benedict Anderson's study of nations as "imagined communities" has identified the paradox of the concept of the nation, or region for that matter. He writes that

> the members of even the smallest nation will never know most of their fellow-members, meet them, or even hear of them, yet in the minds of each lives the image of their communion.
>
> (Anderson 2006: 6)

The imagined community will find its expression in many ways, which includes linguistic ways, whether via attested features (linguistic behaviour) or enregistered (linguistic perceptions and cognitive associations) ones.

The term "enregisterment" is a key concept in the debate, yet has not been mentioned. It goes back to the social anthropologist Asif Agha (2007) and can be defined as the "process by which sets of linguistic forms become ideologically linked with social identities" (Johnstone 2011: 657). It is important to note that any variable can become enregistered and that the process does not depend on actually attested linguistic behaviour; it does not hurt if a group uses a given feature frequently or predominantly, but *use* is only part of the equation. For instance, the discourse marker *eh* has become enregistered as Canadian since the 1960s, while relatively few Canadians use it compared to what public and private discourse might suggest. Pragmatic *right*, by comparison, is four times more frequent than *eh* in Toronto (Denis 2013: Figure 5.3), so *eh* is not ubiquitous. Yet to say that *eh* is not Canadian because the behavioural data do not support it (as pluri-arealists would, following their logic) would be missing an important point—indeed, early in the enregisterment of *eh*, Walter Avis missed *eh*'s significance (1972) himself, claiming *eh* was international. It is argued in this book that the dismissal of enregistered variables is another blind spot in the pluri-areal bandwagon.

5.3 The Pluri-Arealist Bias

What has surprisingly not been acknowledged is the truism that not just pluricentrism may have its ideological bias, but also pluri-areality. The picture that is usually presented is that pluri-areal approaches are exclusively bottom-up, purely linguistic and focused on linguistic behaviour and thus "objective", which is of course not correct. Pluri-areality is at least implicitly based on the idea that one German standard applies to all German speakers in all nations. This ONE STANDARD GERMAN AXIOM finds methodological expression in unrealistically high benchmarks, benchmarks of categoricity that are enforced exclusively on the younger standards, such as Austrian and Swiss German, or possibly Belgian Dutch, without questioning the established German German or Dutch Dutch standard and their historical bases.

Scheuringer expresses the pluri-areal assumptions the clearest. Under the heading "German is a pluri-areal language", Scheuringer claims the following:

> The past few years have more and more shown that the term pluricentric does not adequately reflect the areal patterns of the German language. Initially, the concept has made some positive contributions, at least on the academic level, towards the dissolution of a monocentric view of standard German, including a preference of "Inner-German"

(Binnendeutsch), the de facto mid- and northern German norm; however, its application to German-speaking nations has not brought pluralism, but multiple centrism.

(Scheuringer 1996: 151)

What do we gain if a level of organization with which the vast majority of Austrians identify with, i.e. the national level, is abolished on the grounds that pluricentricity "only" produces three full linguistic centres, and several half and quarter centres in German? It is no gain at all, because the alternatively proposed pluri-areal divisions in German, which are based on a two dozen a priori designed dialect zones (e.g. Elspaß & Niehaus 2014), are not on the same standing as a standard variety, of which there is only one in the pluri-areal design: the German German standard. Pluri-arealists are fully aware that German German—"deutsche[s] Standarddeutsch" counts as grammatically "unmarked" (Dürscheid, Elspaß & Ziegler 2011: 129).

A glance at current textbooks on German dialectology reveals the inadequate consideration of the linguistic identities of the speakers. For a German identity, as the default model, such reasoning might work, but it does not apply to Austrians, Swiss and Liechtensteiners nor to South Tyroleans or East Belgians. Most puzzling perhaps, Schmidt and Herrgen (2011) do not use the term *national variety* at all. Austrian German and Swiss German are therein demoted to supraregional non-standard varieties under a German German standard, as depicted in Figure 4.2. Since the national dimension cannot be fully ignored, one will find opaque terms such as "Oralisierungsnorm" (oral pronunciation norm) and the idea that the same German German standard is realized in different phonetic/phonological ways in Austria and Switzerland, thereby deviating from the standard, which is, of course, German German. The authors subscribe to the idea of a teleological riddance of dialect features, of dialect erosion, and therefore speak merely of "regional dialectal residue" ("Restarealität"). Their book offers no answers, at least no positive ones, to German speakers outside of Germany, while it claims to cover the entire language area.

A note should be added about Austrian literature, the existence of which was questioned some 20 years ago in a similar manner to what we currently see with Standard Austrian German. Not too long ago, Wendelin Schmidt-Dengler defended Austrian literature, writing that "in any case"

it needs to be insisted that there is indeed an Austrian literature that one can refer to and that it is a principle of academic thoroughness and fairness to consider the development of an Austrian literature in its [German literature's] context.

(Schmidt-Dengler 1995: 49)

In this context, it is important to note that some scholars have aimed to define an "Austrian literary German" (e.g. Schrodt 2012). The concept is considerably older, though, and dates back to the early days of World War I. As Willy Haas characterized the writer Franz Werfel, who, like Kafka, was raised in the German-speaking community in Prague, then part of the Austrian–Hungarian Empire and a linguistic centre of German:

> There may no longer have been [in 1914–1915] a real Austria, but there were individuals who possessed an Austrian feeling, an Austrian tradition, an Austrian kind of poetry & writing, even an Austrian language, which was not, in any way, like the one of the German Reich. Of all these, Werfel possessed a lot.
>
> (Haas 1969: 10)

Ammon (1995: 124) makes a similar point interpreting a statement by the German linguist Otto Behagel, who in 1915 saw Austrian and Bavarian varieties as equivalent, but different "in the higher realms of the written language, triggered by special local and historical circumstances in the Danubian empire [Austria]". All this, of course, is wiped out with one stroke if the ONE STANDARD GERMAN AXIOM is accepted.

When pluricentrists are accused of ideological or political bias, quite unfairly so, it is apparently forgotten that no language would have developed a standard variety without a political and language ideological dimension. The bias of the pluri-areal approach is a monocentric one that is, surprisingly, not discussed, especially since a substantial body of work has recently been carried out in a pluri-areal mindset. Is a language standard political? Yes, it is. But it is just as political to propose a Standard Austrian German as it is to promote the ONE STANDARD GERMAN AXIOM. The former expresses an Austrian identity, while the other expresses different ideas that the linguists working with such concepts would need to justify to themselves; one might wonder if they could.

5.4 Reinterpreting Auer (2005)

As we have seen, existing relative similarities of the Upper Austrian and Bavarian dialects gave rise to the pluri-areal stance. The idea is proposed that there is no meaningful border, especially in the context of the European Union, and that the political border is no linguistic border. Until about 1800 and for some time afterwards, this may have been true, but not since. The Canada–US example in British Columbia and Washington State proves the point, which is that international borders, however permeable, do have linguistic impacts. Border regions often remain at the periphery and often increase their linguistic differences with other areas *because* of the open border (e.g. Labov, Ash & Boberg 2005; Dollinger 2012a; Sadlier-Brown 2012).

The second frequently levied charge against pluricentric approaches is the fact that internal variation exists in Austria. In Austria, the dialects of the province of Vorarlberg and small parts of Tyrol are Alemannic German dialects, while the rest of the country speaks Middle Bavarian or Southern Bavarian varieties. Scheuringer (1990a) uses this fact to negate the possibility of Standard Austrian German, while internal variation may be found in any state, including Germany. The result is the postulation of "supraregional varieties", which are identical with traditional dialect zones. To little surprise, Scheuringer's data is claimed to show "in the overwhelming number of cases [. . .] the route towards the development of supraregional varieties" (p. 425) and not an Austrian standard. Rejecting the notion of national standards and with it the entire theory of pluricentricity, Scheuringer still needs to account for cross-border differences, which he attributes to his undefined, ad-hoc "supraregional" varieties.

Supraregional variants are proposed to be aligned with the major cities of Munich (Bavaria) and Vienna (Austria). No rationale is offered, however, as to how a Viennese supraregional dialect is distinguished from Standard Austrian German. I see them both as one and the same and the former as a monocentricity-friendly term. Pluricentric theory predicts that Austrian dialects are influenced by Standard Austrian German, which itself has a considerable Viennese base. Rather than proposing new, undefined terms, Scheuringer might have adopted a pluricentric perspective and used the term Standard Austrian German instead.

The effect of Scheuringer's assessment went far beyond the particular context. Peter Auer's stimulating (2005) paper on political borders in German includes one inconsistency, a non sequitur that is based on Scheuringer's analysis. Using the concepts of convergence and divergence, Auer innovatively schematizes the situation along the Germanic dialect continuum between the Rhineland (German) and the Netherlands (Dutch) that was disrupted by the German–Dutch border in the late sixteenth century and the creation of a Dutch and German standards. Figure 5.1 depicts that the border creates divergence across it, while the dialects on either side tend to converge towards one another. Advergence is another name for "roofing", the linguistic reference points, which since about 1600, have been Standard Dutch and Standard (German) German, respectively.

In Figure 5.1 is in line with the pluricentric development of a new standard variety, which in this case is called a new language. By contrast, Auer's depiction of the Austrian–German border, which cuts across another Germanic dialect continuum, is modelled very differently. This border is modelled as shown in Figure 5.2.

At this point, Auer's text takes over Scheuringer's misinterpretation: The concepts of Standard German German and Standard Austrian German are *not* used as the roof, the adstrate, a function that is assigned to the citylects of Munich and Vienna. We see Scheuringer's supraregional varieties resurface in Auer's work, yet there is no rationale for this step in Scheuringer's

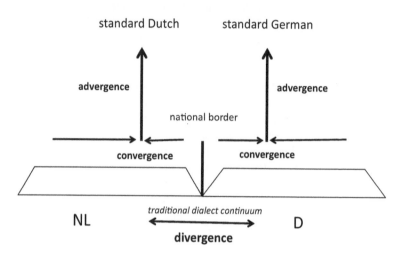

Figure 5.1 Auer's (2005) model at the D-NL border

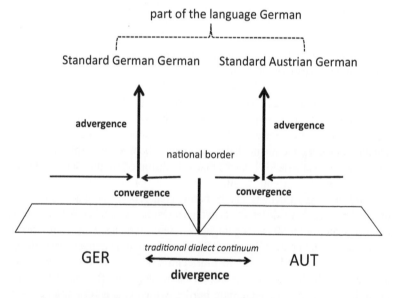

Figure 5.2 Auer's (2005) model at the AUT-D border

Source: based on Scheuringer (1990a)

work. What is clear is that the use of two standard varieties of German as reference points was avoided without a rationale.

The proposition of an "Austrian regional standard" is a dubious construct and yet it is the key concept to prevent the universal "approval" of a

Standard Austrian German. The obvious question must be: what are the reasons for differential modelling? Here are the facts: there are two Germanic dialect continua, the Dutch–Western German continuum and the Austrian German–German German continuum. The former was divided politically and codified in two standards from the sixteenth to the nineteenth centuries; the latter was divided, if we take the ÖWB as a starting point in 1951, harking back to an earlier Imperial history that was disrupted around 1750 (section 2.3). There are two linguistically arbitrary borders, identical cases, yet they are very differently modelled. The reason seems to lie in the ONE STANDARD GERMAN AXIOM that has, unacknowledged, become the default assumption in German dialectology.

The super-regional varieties are sociolinguistically doubtful for Munich and Vienna, as both cities feature profound social differences. The cities are not comparable in terms of international standing and importance for their respective countries. In that regard, Vienna would be Austria's Berlin; note that no one proposes for Berlin a "regional Berlin standard variety" rather than Standard (German) German as a reference point *instead* of the standard. The concept of an "Austrian regional standard" in Figure 5.3 is a construct that would a priori rule out Standard Austrian German, cementing the pre-World War II status in perpetuity. There is no convincing reason why the NL/D situation should be modelled differently from the AUT/GER situation. Figure 5.2, by contrast, conceptualizes the AUT/GER situation with two standard varieties in an inherently consistent and socially realistic depiction of the Austrian–German border.

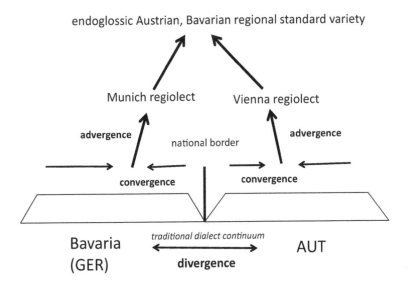

Figure 5.3 The Austrian–German border in the pluricentric framework

Figure 5.2 is consistent with the language attitudes of speakers of Austrian German, as will be shown in Chapter 7. There is no qualitative difference between the concept of two standard varieties developing from a dialect continuum—like German and Dutch—or two standard varieties of the same language developing from the same. Both varieties, autonomous language and autonomous standard variety, derive from a dialect continuum and serve language-identificational functions in their respective countries. The modelling in Figure 5.2 is consistent with pluricentric theory and is found in many language contexts, including Canadian English and American English (e.g. Dollinger 2008).

The resistance against the model in Figure 5.2 is problematic. Schmidlin, Wyss and Davies (2017) summarize the resistance in linguistic circles in the following way, distancing themselves from it:

> When proponents of the pluricentric approach, who themselves come mostly from smaller linguistic centres, use the model to address economical, linguistic and discursive dominance of the Federal German centre, it is interpreted as a protest of the linguistically dominated ones, which may be paired with nationally motivated linguistic purism.
>
> (Schmidlin, Wyss & Davies 2017: 16)

The described reaction, which seems accurate, is indeed puzzling from a linguistic point of view. Wouldn't it be more fitting to say that the proponents hailing mostly from linguistically dominant centres seem to insist on their centre's dominance in spite of widely accepted sociolinguistic core values? Pluri-areality, as an anti-pluricentric idea, has become their vehicle towards maintaining that hegemony.

5.5 Pluricentricity: Outdated in a Borderless Europe vs. *homo nationalis*?

Another point of critique against pluricentrism is that it allegedly fails to consider European integration since 1995, when Austria joined the European Union (EU). This point is remarkable for pluri-arealists who attack political stances in linguistics, as the argument is centred around the profoundly political notion of political union. The clearest proponent of this line of view is Manfred Glauninger, writing that:

> The most recent political trend in the context of European integration indicates that Clyne's concept of national varieties of pluricentric languages is (cf. Clyne 1989, especially: 359)—at least on European soil—becoming anachronistic.
>
> (Glauninger 2001: 172)

The idea that the EU would render the national varieties of German obsolete or "anachronistic" stands out, as comparable super-national units have generally resulted not in a *decrease* but an *increase* of socio-symbolic identity markers, including linguistic variants. In the Canadian context, the post-World War II period has led to ever increasing economic ties with the US, speeding up in the 1960s, long before the EU was gaining momentum. The North American Free Trade Agreement (NAFTA), which went into effect in 1994, shows that increases in economic (the prime pillar in the EU), cultural, and security connections do *not* lead to *fewer* expressions of linguistic identity, but to *more*. Canada–US integration did not just start in 1994, however. Boberg summarizes more than half a century of increasing Canada–US exchanges, writing that

> Canadian English is not on the verge of disappearance in a continental blend dominated by American speech patterns. Despite the massive influence of American English over the last half-century, exercised through increasingly powerful channels like television and the internet, regional linguistic variation remains one of the few ways in which Canadians can still be reliably distinguished from Americans, at least in most parts of the continent.
>
> (Boberg 2010: 250)

From an interactional point of view, an increase of linguistic expression of identity makes sense as speakers signal, simply and easily via language, their roots and identities. Especially for non-dominant countries, the symbolic expressions of identity are often the most effective ones: so, *tap* for Canadians (not *faucet*) and *Jänner* ("January") for Austrians, not *Januar*. It's a question of identity in the international context, where traditional dialects cannot be used; only standard varieties can.

Identity questions are very important in the context of Austria and Austrian German. As Wolfgang Dressler put it in his very positive review of Ammon (1995):

> At least as far as Austria is concerned (where I am most competent), Ammon's [1995] evaluations and judgments are fair and well-balanced. He shows no traces of a "German German language imperialism" vis-a-vis the other national varieties of German, which is very much resented in Austria and Switzerland.
>
> (Dressler 1997: 609–610)

If one uses, in the wintertime, *Haube* and not *Mütze*, i.e. "hat", one uses a Standard Austrian term that is by and large comprehensible to Germans and

Swiss, yet signals simultaneously one's Austrian connection. If such variants are viewed, most often by speakers from Germany, not as legitimate Austrian standard forms but as provincial, rural or quaint, it would be an instance of the "German German language imperialism" that Dressler refers to.

Until Europe has a genuine EU democracy of citizens in which the needs of the smaller nations are duly considered, I do not see any danger for the pluricentricity of German to render itself obsolete. And even then, with the Canadian example serving as a pattern, it is most likely that identification via linguistic means, because of its ease, universality and "low-cost" factor, will likely increase with more integration to reflect the speakers' need to express affiliations internationally.

At present, however, there is no danger for national identity marking to decrease. On the contrary, as the EU has not been following its founding principles, it is presently in bad shape. Few would have predicted only a decade ago that the EU, which was created first and foremost as an antidote to the throes of war, would run into serious trouble because of a migration stream. But the warning signs have been there for a while, so much so that a more general lack of solidarity among the EU nations has only shown how quickly democratic foundations may become volatile. The EU has so far been more a union of bureaucrats than citizens, and Glauninger's reasoning is along those bureaucratic lines that forget to consider the people, while they dream of a unified Europe. As historian Tom Segev put it recently:

> We don't have that [a unified Europe] because the national feelings are still very strong. It's not something that is over. There was a phase, perhaps 20 years ago, when people thought it's over.
>
> (Segev 2018)

That "national feelings are still very strong" is not difficult to discern in today's populist movements. Even 20 years ago, however, the dream of a unified Europe entailed a long and difficult road; for good reason, Wodak et al. (2009: 4) speak of Europeans as *homo nationalis*, referring to identities that are co-determined by national dimensions. Likewise, Crystal (2017: 331) talks about "country-focused" social conventions and a lack of a cultural EU identity. The latter is uncertain to arise. Seidlhofer and Widdowson (2017: 361), for instance, consider the "likelihood of a common European identity developing at all" as "questionable" in the light of "the continuing historical adherence to the idea of separate nation-states". There are German, Austrian, Swedish, Danish, Norwegian, Dutch and Belgian identities that need to be expressed, which must not be conflated with rabid nationalism. Once that is accepted, the member states can embark on the construction of a European identity that is borne by the population at large.

Our colleagues in the historical disciplines have been more aware of underlying trends and skewed perceptions than we seem to have been in sociolinguistics. In a brilliant paper on the role of the Holy Roman Empire in the consciousness of the German people, Joachim Whaley repeatedly raises a point in German historical research that seems relevant to the negative role that national dimensions are given in German linguistics. Summarizing dominant intellectual trends, Whaley blames "decades of West German 'post-national' thinking" as resulting in a "diminished sensitivity to the continuing significance of national issues for many neighbouring countries" (Whaley 2002: 35). These neighbouring countries include Austria, despite a profoundly joint history with Germany that is now a distant past. It is impossible to stress this past culturally or linguistically, as the pluri-areal paradigm does, without negating Austrian identities. While "post-national" may be a default intellectual stance in Germany, it cannot negate the identities of other EU member states. It is entirely possible that "pluri-areality" is the brainchild of Whaley's detected "diminished sensitivity".

6   The Case Against "Pluri-Areality"

It is time to probe the monocentric pluri-areal concept. There are five points of criticism against pluri-areality; considered together, they show the problems with an approach that cannot adequately replace pluricentric theory.

6.1 Demystifying Pluri-Areality = "Geographical Variation"

It is fair to say that pluri-areality has never been specified beyond the simple fact that it is an anti-pluricentric notion. Some 25 years after its introduction, pluri-areality still lacks definition. De Cillia and Ransmayr (forthcoming) address the "noticeable" fact "that the [pluri-areal] approach is in comparison with pluricentric ones theoretically little elaborated" (de Cillia & Ransmayr forthcoming: section 5.3). They identify as missing the

> explication of the basic axiomatic assumptions and hypotheses concerning the connection of linguistic and extralinguistic variables, the development of a clearly defined terminological apparatus (as is available [for pluricentric approaches] in Ammon 1995), and its methodological approaches.
>
> (de Cillia & Ransmayr forthcoming: section 5.3)

For pluricentricity, the monographs by Clyne (1995) and Ammon (1995: 117–227 for Austria) serve this purpose. The wholesale endorsement of a very vague term in lieu of a well-established concept in German dialectology is, not least from a scientific and historical point of view, astounding.

The following passage comes as close to a definition of pluri-areality as any other. We see that the notion is tied to Austria and is used as a signpost that is left undefined:

> Especially in relation to the standard language in Austria it is areal patterns, e.g. the old Bavarian–Austrian area, or the area that defines

a general southern German, that are much more frequent than the nation-bound areas or smaller areas that operate below the level of the nation state. Yet more frequent, outright overwhelmingly so, is "One-Areality" [i.e. where no regional variation exists at all]. One-Areality is, it needs to be said, the base of a functioning and practicable Hochsprache [standard language]. Because One-Areality is, just as the nation-oriented pluricentric pattern, not the only pattern, the German language is pluri-areal.

(Scheuringer 1996: 152)

The passage includes the characteristic ad-hoc labelling—"One-Areality" (German original: "Einräumlichkeit"), without definitions. De Cillia and Ransmayr (forthcoming) summarize the "pluri-areal" stance

as a conceptual and language-planning counter stance, without offering a theoretical elaboration, respectively a systematic inventory of terms similar to what the pluricentric approach has developed for analytical reasons.

How can it be, one might wonder, that we still do not know what "pluri-areality" entails? The reason is surprisingly simple and logical but has taken a long time to establish: "pluri-areality" is merely another term for *geographical variation*. Since every language varies over geographical distances, "pluri-areality" is an empty concept, a non-concept. Readers approaching pluri-areal literature by replacing "pluri-areal" with "geographical variation" will see that this simple point holds water: pluri-areal is a synonym for geographical variation. Try a few passages from the most recent literature (e.g. Elspaß, Dürscheid & Ziegler 2017; Lenz 2018); they will all work and make perfect sense with the substitution "pluri-areal" = (in German) "geografisch".

If researchers are against pluricentricity, they need to say so and offer their reasons. Yet the invention of a new term that does not add any theoretical or descriptive knowledge does nothing more than hinder meaningful discussion. A linguistic theory, as any theory, should make predictions about language variation that are testable: pluricentricity does. Pluri-areality (geographical variation) does not.

Had Scheuringer said in 1990 that he did not believe in national varieties for reasons X, Y and Z and that he preferred to operate with the neutral term "geographical variation" in lieu of pluricentricity, one would from the outset have recognized that Scheuringer operates atheoretically. But the adoption of the term "pluri-areality", which implies something different than merely geographical variation—some kind of theory that it does not offer—is nothing but misleading and should not be part of academic knowledge creation.

After all, since we teach our first years to define their terms, we should do lead by example. What example do "pluri-arealists" offer?

6.2 Atheoretical Empiricism

The past 20 years have seen a most welcome focus on non-standard data in historical linguistics. In the case of English, such refocusing included the study of non-British and non-American data in "alternative histories" of English (Watts & Trudgill 2002). The new discipline of historical sociolinguistics has unearthed atypical and neglected sources, such as private letters and ego documents, that have broadened available perspectives (e.g. Elspaß et al. 2007; Auer, Schreier & Watts 2015). One approach is a "bottom-up" or "from below" approach, that is, working from non-standard, often lower-class data, and building up one's conclusions from the data. Pluri-arealists claim to take an approach to language "from below", i.e. including non-print and vernacular texts. This may work in some contexts, though from the scientific–theoretical aspect, the approach is more problematic than first meets the eye. In the area of standard-language modelling, a bottom-up approach is questionable if it is applied in an etic, i.e. an outsider, perspective. What is missing is the acknowledgement that a "bottom up" approach must be anchored in theory and that it is per se not better than any "top-down" approach with theory. Bottom-up approaches, if carried out uncritically, may fare worse than well-reasoned top-down ones. While a wider range of data is desirable, it cannot replace theory and predictions that are testable and actually being tested.

6.2.1 Description, Theory and Lack Thereof

The most important difference between pluricentricity and pluri-areality is the role of theory. The former offers clear predictions, while the latter is merely another name for geographical variation and does not offer any predictions. Pluricentricity, for instance, predicts that across a border region, such as in Braunau (Austria) and Simbach (Germany), or in Vancouver (Canada) and Bellingham or Seattle (USA), speech patterns diverge over time. It also stipulates that the dialects of neighbouring towns on each side of the border would converge with one another.

By contrast, pluri-areal stances are atheoretical approaches to language in space. By claiming that German is a pluri-areal language, one merely says that there is geographical variation of some sort but nothing else. While a comprehensive theory of linguistic space does not yet exist, important building blocks do. In key papers on the topic, Britain (2002, 2010) distinguishes between geographical space, social space and perceived space. Traditional dialect geography has been limited to mapping geographical space with linguistic variables, often in the form of isoglosses.

Chambers and Trudgill (1998: 104–123) studied transition zones and connected the geographical with the social dimensions. Scheuringer's study and most pluri-areal approaches, however, only consider geographical space with no consideration of social and perceived space, which would bring the role of the political border into focus. Such perspectives also fail to consider existing social networks and how cross-border social space is patterned, including questions such as whether Braunauers travel to Simbach and if so, for what reasons, or whether there is a lot of cross-border dating and the like. It also does not include "perceived space", i.e. one's subjective interpretations of space, e.g. do Braunauers consider themselves as feeling, acting or perhaps sounding differently from the Simbachers? Is their group friendlier, more indirect or the like, which requires an emic, in-group perspective that I have not seen in pluri-areal approaches? The social and perceptual (cognitive) dimensions are important sociolinguistic dimensions that inform enregisterment, or the lack thereof. These dimensions have been conspicuously absent in pluri-areal work and, if applied, are applied from a monocentric angle (section 7.2).

6.2.2 The Pluri-Areal Dilemma: Popper's Missing Falsification

A key point against pluri-areality is rooted in its proponents' empirical method, which is generally stressed as "new" and "up-to-date" (Glauninger 2013: 131), as reflecting linguistic variation "more adequately" (*gerechter*) (Elspaß, Engel & Niehaus 2013: 59), as "empirical" (Dürscheid, Elspaß & Ziegler 2011: 135), with "fewer presuppositions" (*weniger strikte Vorannahmen*) (Niehaus 2017: 64), as "advantageous" and as generally "more flexible" (Niehaus 2017: 64) than the pluricentric model. It is indeed so "flexible" that it fails to meet minimal theoretical requirements.

There is the real danger in any data-driven, bottom-up approach that operates without theory that the analyst sees in the data what one is used to seeing. If that analyst has not been socialized in Austria, where a rich social and geographical dialect continuum is operational, the analyst will need to take extra care to draw adequate conclusions (as the author knows from Canada). If socialized in Austria, however, the analyst would bring other biases to the task (as I know from Canada, too). The difference is that in good studies theory must be clearly expressed and exposed to falsification. In pluri-areal studies, the data is made to fit the pluri-areal frame. The implicit connection of "pluriareality" with "bottom-up" and "from below", while "pluricentricity" is associated with "top-down", "idealization" or "from above", is science–theoretically incorrect. It is much like considering corpus linguistics (bottom-up) as opposed to cognitive linguistics (top-down), while in actual fact the good corpus linguists approach their data with (cognitive) theory in mind to test their theoretically derived hypotheses on their corpus data.

What can be done about this problem? Karl Popper, perhaps the most prominent scholar of the theory of science, makes very basic points in his 1934 monograph *Logik der Forschung* (*The Logic of Research*). One of his famous dicta is the following:

> There is fundamentally no end to the game of science: those who decide one day to no longer test their scientific findings and consider them as verified, are leaving the game.
>
> (Popper 1966 [1934]: 26)

What Scheuringer (e.g. 1996), Elspaß and Niehaus (2014), Herrgen (2015) and others have in common is that they, by rejecting pluricentricity, no longer work with a theory, as pluri-areality is not a theoretical concept but at best a mildly descriptive term (= geographical variation). They choose to trust, in violation of Popper's basic principle of theory-based testing, in the data alone and to use the data to justify the ONE STANDARD GERMAN AXIOM.

As Popper tells us, what is possible is description *either with a clearly expressed theory* or *with an unexpressed theory*. Editors of linguistic atlases or big dictionary projects are prey to this problem for the amounts of data they have to juggle, so it often happens that the theory is not properly attended to (see Dollinger 2016b). The lack of an acknowledgement or perhaps the refusal of the possibility of a Standard Austrian German that is on a par with Standard German German seriously limits any theoretical approaches. As a consequence, Scheuringer is forced to perform odd conceptual twists and turns to make programmatic statements:

> Isn't it the case that a linguist is supposed to simply describe the interesting cases of areality in our case [. . .] on all its levels such as traditional dialect, Umgangssprache, written language etc.?
>
> (Scheuringer 1996: 147)

The above statement is a frank acknowledgment of the fallacy of description without theory: "to simply describe" and to dispense with theory is at the core of the pluri-areal dilemma. An analyst will inevitably be approaching the data in a biased way, because only theory can offer independent fail-safes. The theory-based falsification of hypotheses may be a cumbersome and slow method, but it is the only one that works to prevent bias. Because of a lack of an explicit theory, the notion of "Ein-Räumlichkeit", or "one-area-ness", in the German language becomes Scheuringer's implicit theoretical base and the base of the pluri-areal camp in German dialectology today (see section 6.5).

It is of course possible that pluricentricity as a theoretical concept cannot meet all demands of description, but to abandon it for the theoretically empty term of "pluri-areality" brings us back to a pre-Popperian approach in dialectology. "Pluri-areality" merely says there is regional variation, while the ONE STANDARD GERMAN AXIOM enters through the backdoor. As Labov, Ash and Boberg (2005) pointed out in their *Atlas of North American English*: it "is now generally recognized that theory cannot be avoided so easily" (2006: 4). And theory is, unexpressed, at the base of "pluri-areality" in the form of what I call the ONE STANDARD GERMAN AXIOM, which is firmly rooted in a German German standard.

6.3 The Axiom of Categoricity

Given the critique offered so far, it is doubtful how the pluri-areal take can be applied to non-dominant national verities without the distortion of speaker realities. The concept that allows such distortions to happen is what Chambers (2009) calls the Axiom of Categoricity. Originally found in generative linguistics, we see in many "pluri-arealist" interpretations clear signs of adopting the Axiom of Categoricity into sociolinguistics, the very discipline that was developed in critique to categoricity in generative linguistics.

What does the Axiom proclaim? It says that if you have theory X and if you find a single case that does not fit theory X, then theory X is to be discarded. This, of course, is nonsense in probabilistic linguistics, where it is about getting as close as possible to predicting all cases, knowing that this will never come about. Often, a rate of 30% or more in predictive power is considered "sound" in the social sciences.

Not so for the pluri-arealists, as the next example shows. If one looks at the distribution of the pronunciation of the final vowel in *Kaffee* ("coffee"), one will find, near-categorically, a *long* /e:/ in Austria and a short /e/ in almost all of Germany, with Switzerland pretty much in the German pattern. Figure 6.1 shows the distributions in Austria, Switzerland and Germany from pluri-areal sources. Monocentrists would now argue that some long /e:/s are used in Switzerland and in some Bavarian border regions, and one short /e/ is found in Vienna, so that long /e:/ is not "absolute" in Austria and is therefore a case *against* pluricentricity. Such interpretations hinge on categoricity and throw the proverbial baby out with the bathwater: questions would need to be asked, such as who are the speakers that in Bavaria use a long /e:/? Do they have ties with Austria? Perhaps they work in Salzburg or have an Austrian girlfriend and circle of friends? Still, the fact that there are outliers does not falsify the theory of pluricentricity. On the contrary, the nice alignment of the reported data with the international border is a good case *for* pluricentricity.

The case of *Kaffee*, a stereotypical Austrian variable that is tied to Austrian coffeehouse tradition, is not the only case in which categoricity is used to refute Austrian claims to national linguistic identity. Elspaß and Niehaus

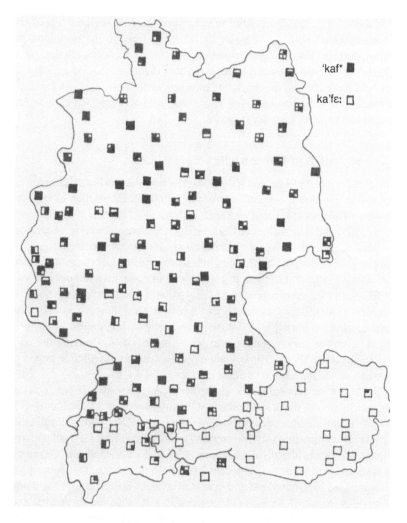

Figure 6.1 Secondary students' pronunciation of *Kaffee*
Source: Schmidt and Herrgen (2011: 367)

(2014: 56), for instance, present grammatical variation in verbs, i.e. the order in subordinate clauses of the finite verb, the auxiliary verb and the lexical verb. The patterns can be

> *dass er werden kann gesehen (1–2–3)*
> *dass er gesehen werden kann (3–1–2)*
> *dass er kann gesehen werden (2–3–1)*

The results from an online questionnaire, though showing some methodological limitations, are nevertheless quite clear. They are summarized as follows:

> The 3–1–2 (*gesehen werden kann*) order is very noticeable in the southeastern regions of the German-speaking language area. In Austria, it is even the dominant (but not absolute) variant. As leading grammar books such as the Duden grammar consider themselves grammars of usage, it is surprising that the 3–1–2 variant has not been marked as a standard variant yet.
>
> (Elspaß & Niehaus 2015: 56, English in the original)

For the linguist of Austrian German, it is of course not surprising that the Duden Grammar (or dictionary) does not list many Austrian standard constructions, as its northern German bias has long been a cause of concern (see section 5.1). Given the above summary, however, one would not imagine that the depiction, using the percentage responses from the survey, would look like Figure 6.2.

What sounds like a case against pluricentrism in Elspaß and Niehaus' words looks in Figure 6.2 again very much like a case *in its favour*. The dark bar is pattern 3–1–2, standing out with 90% or more in Austria in all locations and only to about 10% in most of Germany and less in Switzerland. Only one region of Bavaria uses 3–1–2 as a large minority form of about 30%, while the major pattern is the ECG standard of 2–3–1.

The Bavarian outlier is utterly predictable if that region is treated as a transition zone between the Austrian standard and the German (ECG) standard, as Chambers and Trudgill (1998: 104–123) first theorized. In the transition zone, usage has not yet settled, but it no longer matches the levels for 3–1–2 seen in Austria. Pluricentricity theory predicts that the original dialects are pushed back further in Germany as a result of the roofing of Standard German, with 1–2–3, *werden kann gesehen*, as the major variant; consequently, one will find less of the original 3–1–2 pattern in Bavaria, where it has already decreased considerably as a result of German language roofing. In Austria, the roofing standard is Austrian, where 3–1–2 is codified. What is missing in Elspaß and Niehaus' interpretation is both a diachronic angle and a theoretical angle in relation to border studies and transition zones.

This case is clearly in favour of pluricentricity, showing core zones (centres in pluricentricity) in Austria and in Germany, and a transition zone in Bavaria, as a result of the shorter existence of the border. While there are other cases that are not as clear, for instance, the verb sequences of *hätte wissen müssen*, such cases do not falsify, as is usually claimed, the pluricentric approach, because it does not operate on the assumption of categoricity. If categoricity, in fact, were of any relevance in sociolinguistics, it

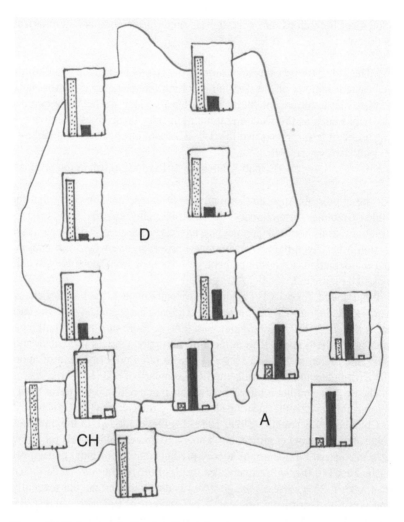

Figure 6.2 Verb sequence in subordinate clauses
Source: Elspaß and Niehaus (2014: 55)

would have rendered the formation and codification of Norwegian illusive. As Haugen summarizes, variation was found within Norway and features were shared across the border with Sweden and Denmark:

the historical evidence clearly showed that development [of linguistic variation] even within the country had been divergent, while there were contacts across political boundaries with neighboring Sweden and Denmark from the earliest times [a geographical dialect continuum with Sweden, SD].

(Haugen 1966: 300)

In the Canadian–US context, there are many examples of variants that are used in both Canada and the US, or parts of each. *Sneakers* for "running shoe", for instance, is the majority term in the US and also in Maritime Canada, while from the province of Quebec westwards, the majority term is *runners* or *running shoes* (Chambers 1998). No one, however, disputes the existence of a Canada–US isogloss because of such cases. Why, then, is there discussion about Austrian German?

There are Canadian examples where the border coincides with linguistic isoglosses, including more recent innovations such as *cube van* ("moving truck"; Dollinger 2015b) or *take up* ("go over test answers"; Dollinger 2017). By contrast, the existence of a Standard Austrian German is negated in "pluri-arealist" thinking because some Bavarians say *Rauchfang* ("chimney"), like almost all Austrians do (and not *Schornstein*, the more German choice); because some Austrians today say *Metzger* for butcher, where they used to say almost categorically *Fleischhauer, -hacker*. Is the reason the "Germanization" of Austrian German? Hardly. A socially sensitive explanation will discover that some Austrians switch, because Austrian *Fleischhauers* have discovered that they can charge more if they market themselves as *Metzgers*. A *Fleischhauer* is coded as [+ordinary] in Austria, while a Metzger, slightly exotic, can be considered [+upscale]. And if *Metzger* is on the sign, you are likely to repeat it when referring to the store (and be billed more).

In the recent second edition of the *Dictionary of Canadianisms on Historical Principles* (Dollinger & Fee 2017, in short DCHP-2), we have tried hard to falsify all claims for terms, meanings and expressions to be Canadian (by the definition in Dollinger 2015b). The result is an open access dictionary at www.dchp.ca/dchp2. DCHP-2 is built on a pluricentric framework but not, as Sutter (2017) suggests, because the approach is simpler. On the contrary, most variables were discovered *because of* our pluricentric approach (Auer, Hinskens & Kerswill 2005; Dollinger 2016a), while a pluri-areal perspective and methodology would have smoothed over them.

Despite a recent uptake of the idea, the pluri-areal camp has at least one prominent dissenter. Heinz-Dieter Pohl has recently clarified his position in Pohl (1997) on Austrian German, which he considers a national variety in its own right:

I therefore consider Austrian German a national variety as a result of historical sovereignty [. . .]. I am therefore of the opinion that the regional patterns, as they exist in German on a big scale, are matched in Austria on a smaller scale. It is beyond dispute that some variables are limited to Austria alone, though such only rarely cover the entire area of Austria.

(Pohl 2018: 142)

Pohl (2018: 137) defines Standard Austrian German as the "country-specific standardization" of German (ibid.: 130). What can also be seen in the above quote is the requirement of the full state area coverage of linguistic variables, which shows how deep the idea of categoricity runs in German dialectological circles. Categoricity, as we've seen in the previous section, has been used formidably against the formation of non-dominant standard varieties, which shows a double standard that no dominant variety had to meet.

6.4 Type vs. Tokens and Social Salience

A point that is often brought forth against pluricentricity is the "insignificant" number of linguistic differences between two national varieties. How many differences are needed in order for a national variety to appear as "sufficiently different"? It is an interesting and often overlooked fact that linguists do not have an answer to this question. This is because languages and varieties are constructed primarily by social and not by linguistic means. Why is there a Norwegian, Danish and Swedish, for instance? Why an American and a British English? It is not because the linguistic differences between these varieties are "big". It is because of a social consensus that they should be treated as different varieties. Therefore, "pluri-arealist" statements such as "two per cent of variation in standard German lexis and pronunciation" (Elspaß & Niehaus 2014: 50) have no empirical basis but rather show that the pluri-areal approach is a blind, mechanical, asocial approach.

What is lacking in pluri-areal accounts is the basic distinction between types and tokens. By type, we mean an abstract category of a linguistic item, such as the verb PLAY. By token we mean the actual number of realizations of that type in a given context. The pluri-areal counts of what is an "absolute" (categorical) variable; what is "relative" (shared with other varieties) are all based on type counts. Not every variable is equally important in the linguistic identification process. The noun *Jänner*, the Standard Austrian term for January (Ger Ger *Januar*) is just one word, one type, but once a year it occurs a lot, with a lot of tokens in discourse, written and spoken. "Pluri-arealists" are blind to the importance of the type-token ratio: it may just be *one type*, but that one type may be uttered, written, read and heard a billion times, *in a billion tokens*, from about November to February. Even more importantly, what speakers associate with the term is essential—its social salience—not how many terms there are. While the originally German informal good-bye *Tschüss*, sacrilegious to most Austrian German speakers in the 1980s as a foreign term, is now accepted in Austria among the young and thus also Austrian [+young], the situation with *Jänner* is very different.

Regardless of what pluri-arealists claim, the *number* of differences is quite irrelevant. The difference, in fact, may be larger than linguists think, and bigger by comparison than the differences between Canadian and American English or Swedish and Norwegian. But the number of differences, as long as it is 1 or 1+, is quite irrelevant. Estimates about the Austrian character of the lexis, assumed to be the most distinct part, range from around 2% to 20%. Wiesinger (2014: 262) reports a number of 3%, based on 7,000 Austrianisms in a handbook of Austrianisms, and compares it against the 220,000 lexemes found in major dictionaries. Measured against the same base, the percentage of Canadian English would, by comparison, with some 2200 documented terms, not even reach half the Austrian count.

Type counts are meaningless: it is not the count but the use of terms and their social salience that counts. Genetics offers a good analogy. Consider an organism's overall gene count (types) vs. the realizations and effects of particular genes (tokens): humans and chimpanzees share 98% of their genes (types), yet no one would argue that such "small difference" of just 2% does not matter. In like manner, the pluri-arealist stance misses the key point of sociolinguistic differentiation, which is never absolute and static, but socially embedded. Such meaning can only be decoded in the given social context, a context that is co-defined by national constraints. Typologists, who study varieties cross-linguistically, are quite clear on the important type-token distinction:

> The number of features which an area shares is a much-discussed matter in linguistic typology [. . .]. However, the number does not need to be great, and there are cases where single features are involved.
>
> (Hickey 2017: 2)

Muhr (2017: 35) questions the pluri-arealists' low type counts of Austrian lexical features, offering a count of 45,000 Austria-specific lexical items (the upper end of 20% difference), which includes legal language and other text types that are more specialized. Judging from the Canadian experience, there are very intricate uses of linguistic items that have gone unnoticed for decades, as they are impossible to detect without more sophisticated analysis (e.g. Dollinger 2017). While a higher number for distinct Austrian items is likely, the number of variants does, in the sense of Hickey's quote, not matter.

Virtually all pluri-areal studies operate with a selection of variants that are reported in a social void. Schmidlin is one of the few voices in the debate that recognize salience:

> In the case of pluricentric varieties of standard German, the typical features are identical with Austrianisms, Helvetisms and Germanisms and regional variants, which show varying degrees of salience. [. . .] The number of such variants is therefore less important than the inter-relationship of pragmatic, lexical and in case of the spoken standard, phonological markers.
>
> (Schmidlin 2011: 291–292)

Rather than studying variables devoid of social context and resorting to counting and applying subjective cut-off points (2% is not "enough"), the more complete, social assessment of markers of varieties of standard German is needed.

6.5 Formulae in a Black Box

A potentially positive side effect of the pluri-areal approach is that it has promoted a computational angle in German dialectology. The adoption of mathematical models in dialect geography, i.e. an improvement of dialectometric methods, is in the absence of theory both strength and weakness. If the analysts framed their data in a pluricentric framework, they would have independent hypotheses for falsification. In the Popperian sense, we do not speak of verification as only "falsification" or "not-falsification" of a theory-derived hypothesis is possible. Theories are only valid for as long as they are not falsified, but can never be verified—which is the approach taken in DCHP-2 (as a matter of fact, Considine 2017 falsified our classification of *parkade* ("car park") as Canadian in origin. The category of Canadian by virtue of frequency still holds, though; see http://dchp.ca/dchp2/Entries/view/parkade).

In the pluri-areal approach, mathematical methods of simplifying and summarizing the raw data become important. In the absence of explicit theory, the algorithm that is supposed to detect isoglosses is key and the precise algorithm actually becomes synonymous with the theory. One such aggregate method is multidimensional scaling, another dialectometric intensity.

Pluri-arealists have employed dialectometric intensity models, using a simple algorithm that is sensitive to the geographical distances of each location's neighbours to compute dialect zones. This method, like any other abstraction method, systematically distorts dialect boundaries. Common to all aggregate methods is the critique that the behaviour of the underlying linguistic variables "is completely obscured" (Ruette & Speelman 2014: 89).

The pluri-areal method smooths over traditionally established and consensual dialect zones. In the wording of a pluri-arealist technical paper, it

> frequently happens that differences in individual variables that coincide with structural dialect borders are straightened, shifted, or otherwise blurred.
>
> (Pickl et al. 2014: 29)

An alternative method, which uses an algorithm harnessing linguistic differences between variants rather than mere geographical distances, fares somewhat better, yet the problem of appropriate parameter settings remains:

> it is clear that in a different region and with other data, the results could be in favour of other parameter settings or even of geographical distances.
>
> (ibid.: 38)

Such algorithm leaves key decisions in the hands of the analysts, i.e. the parameter settings, which opens the door for any preconceptions and unreflected biases, rendering doubtful any claims to objectivity—"derived from the data itself" (Elspaß, Dürscheid & Ziegler 2017: 71). The general problem with apparently "objective" mathematical models in dialect geography was recognized in Embleton, Uritescu and Wheeler (2013), who changed as a result their mathematical model in a most radical way, by *not* using raw data as input but interpretive data, which "worked better than raw data" (2013: 20). For the interpretative data, and this is key, "a human researcher has reviewed the data, made an assessment of whether or not two locations are the same, and recorded this with symbols" (2013: 17). Embleton and associates rejected, in other words, the pure mechanical approach and introduced a perception angle.

Good data, whether raw or interpretive, is only one part of the equation. Explicit theory offering testable and falsifiable predictions is not just optional, but a second requirement. In this area, the monocentrists show little awareness. Since "pluri-areality" makes no statements as to the role of international borders, it cannot serve as a theoretical concept. Pluricentricity can. Since pluri-areality aims to avoid national varieties, using "default regions" that are set up and distributed across the DACH countries, it cannot serve as a theoretical backdrop of hypothesis testing for national varieties. Pluricentricity can.

While the efforts by Pickl (2013, 2014) and others are welcome, they would benefit from a theoretical angle. Theory-derived testing would bestow much more confidence on crucial decisions, such as which parameter setting is chosen (a problem long acknowledged, e.g. Goebl 1984, 2007). As a result, the pluri-areal approach questions the notion of variety more generally, not just national varieties. As Nerbonne (2015: 126) pointed out within Pickl's (2013) approach, the method appears to "undermine the integrity of the term variety and thus dialect area" itself.

A reasonable and well-defined concept of "variety" is the *sine qua non* in dialectology and in border studies. As we've seen, Embleton, Uritescu and Wheeler (2013) introduced a human soft factor element to ensure its consideration in their model. On the contrary, in pluri-areality the yard-stick of categoricity is held against national varieties, and the mathematical model is used to confirm the unquestioned unmarkedness of German German. Implicitly, the superiority of Standard German German is made the impenetrable benchmark for the assessment of all forms. The theoretical shortcomings of the pluri-areal approach cannot be counter-balanced by the use of mathematical methods. Theory would offer a correction. Another correction would be to take speaker attitudes and perceptions of the supposed national variety seriously. Factoring in linguistic insecurity is a key in such assessments, as most Austrians have to deal with it from the day they go beyond their immediate local settings.

7 The Lynchpin: Speaker Attitudes

> Because we've mentioned the topic [social coherence in Austrian society]:
> I am a fervent European and cosmopolitan but above all I am an unbelieva-
> ble patriot, which sometimes (laughing) gets met into trouble. But I love this
> country [Austria], even if sometimes it's more of a love-hate relationship.
> —Actor Katharina Stemberger (2018)

The present chapter looks at linguistic attitudes of speakers of Austrian German. Attitudinal studies on Austrian German (e.g. Moosmüller 1991; Ransmayr 2006; Pfrehm 2007; de Cillia & Ransmayr forthcoming) and Swiss German (e.g. Schmidlin 2011, 2017) show highly relevant insights into what the speakers consider as "real". Actress Katharina Stemberger, who is quoted above, is certainly a cosmopolitan, liberal person. Yet as her quote demonstrates, she is also an Austrian patriot, to a degree that it puzzles herself. Such attitudes are bound to find their linguistic expressions.

7.1 State Nation Austria vs. Nation State Germany

In the mid-1960s, the Austrian state nation, i.e. a nation formed by consensus rather than ethnicity or "race", showed modest approval rates of around 60%, which underwent steady increases: by 1964 to 64%, by 1970 to 66% and by 1980 to 67%. The early 1990s witnessed a bigger jump: by 1990 to 74%, which increased in 1992 to an approval rating of 80% (Bruckmüller 1994: 15, qtd. in Wiesinger 2000: 556). What is important is that the Austrian national sentiment is often expressed in opposition to the earlier affiliation of belonging to a German nation. The state nation concept is markedly different from the "ethnicity"-inspired (*Volk*) idea of the nation state, where one people constitute a state.

Sociolinguistically, there is solid evidence today that Austrian German is identity-confirming beyond the non-standard level. Wodak et al. (2009: 193) found the "vernacular or dialectal level" is a major identity marker in Austrian German, and identity-marking effects are also found on the standard level. Soukoup's (2013) attitude study in a matched-guise design showed that the use of Standard Austrian German—in comparison to Austrian dialect—is associated by listeners with "higher *intelligence, smartness*, and *competence* than the dialect"; Austrian dialect, by contrast, is perceived as more natural, relaxed, homey, emotional and showing a better sense of humour (Soukoup 2016: 166). De Cillia reasons that

> the German language therefore plays—despite the official understanding [of Austria] as a nation founded by consensual agreement—actually an important role for Austrians' national identity constructions, it has been and is being instrumentalized for identity politics [. . .] and for demarcation with the other German-speaking countries, when the Austrian variety of the German language is set in focus.
>
> (de Cillia 2015: 162)

The concept of a Standard Austrian German clearly serves identity functions. Pfrehm's (2007) study on standard variant acceptance found significant differences in what is perceived as standard in Austria and in Germany:

> looking at standardness, for the ASG [Austrian Standard German] words the Austrians' mean significantly outscored that of the Germans. For the GSG [German Standard German] words, the German respondents scored a significantly higher mean than the Austrians.
>
> (Pfrehm 2007: 53)

In contradiction to these findings, a recent contribution from the Marburg school of dialectology appears to be interpreting decontextualized data in contradiction to the above findings (Herrgen 2015). This study, entitled the "de-nationalization of the standard", demotes Austrian German to the sub-standard level and will be re-analysed below in the context of linguistic insecurity.

7.2 Linguistic Insecurity

It is noticeable that major proponents of German dialectology follow an implicit monocentric approach in the modelling of standard varieties. Herrgen's (2015) paper is a particularly insightful case. It does not just support Scheuringer's interpretations, but takes the One Standard German Axiom to a new level by concluding that an exonormative German standard is fully accepted in Austria and that the "de-nationalization" of German standards has thus begun. That is a strange statement for any speaker of Austrian German.

Herrgen (2015: 139) bases his study on an abstract, a priori monocentric reference point, a "target norm" that "is the communicative orientation of the members of a speech community" (ibid.: 140). Given that all speakers, regardless of their social and national backgrounds, are focusing on just one norm, an underlying bias is exerted. The speech community is left undefined, but implicitly equated with German German, and all members, regardless of provenance, are treated as speakers within an all-German language speech community. Methodologically, hard benchmarks are introduced to classify a speaker as Standard (S), Informal Standard (IS) or Dialect (Di), in disregard of Pfrehm's findings of relative benchmarks. The claim that a regionally perceived speech is identified by an absolute benchmark of just one non-standard word or more for every five words enforces the East Central German standard as "normal" in all three countries from the beginning (ibid.: 140).

Herrgen uses Scheuringer in support of his thesis of the "denationalization" of national varieties of German, considering pluricentrism as a "reduction to the national dimension" (Herrgen 2015: 142). As in Scheuringer, a range of terms is offered also in Herrgen, a feature shared with other pluri-areal papers. Terminology such as "Regionalstandard", supposedly part of the standard, or "Regionalakzent", which is apparently not (e.g. Herrgen 2015: 144), are the twists and turns we know from the post-1985 Scheuringer. While the ad-lib creation of terms is common in this approach, there are severely critical methodological problems with this type of study.

7.2.1. Pluri-Areal Misinterpretations

Herrgen's paper will be probed for its underlying assumptions and its failure to consider the phenomenon of linguistic insecurity in Austria. The concept has a long pedigree (e.g. Owens & Baker 1984) and can be illustrated by the mean scores in Figure 7.1. The code S stands for "Standard", IS for "Intended Standard", presumably speakers who want to reach it but "fail" at it, and "Di" is traditional dialect. Students were asked to act as respondents in three locations, Wien (Vienna, Austria), Freiburg (Switzerland) and Marburg (Germany). The lower the score, the more a speech sample was associated with "Hochdeutsch", which is a highly ambiguous term in Austria but is used as a synonym for standard German of a further undefined quality.

Figure 7.1 shows that the ratings are quite alike in all three locations for S-D, the German German standard, the German German dialects (Di-D) and Swiss German dialects (Di-CH). Among the Viennese students, the German standard speaker, S-D, is considered the most "Hochdeutsch", closely followed by the Austrian standard speaker, S-A. The Marburg students, however, assign the speaker of Standard Austrian German a dialect score of greater than 2, which is interpreted by Herrgen as a "dialectal" speaker. How is it possible, one might ask, that the Marburg students confuse a speaker of Standard Austrian German with a non-standard Austrian

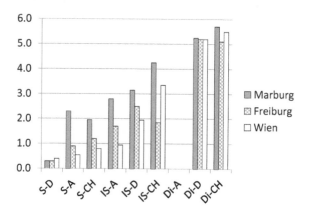

Figure 7.1 Results of Herrgen's perception study (Herrgen 2015: 154)
0 = "pure Hochdeutsch" 6 = "deepest dialect"

dialect speaker? Herrgen finds this "the most surprising result of the present study, which is utterly clear, yet not expected as such" (ibid.: 155). The perception rating is translated directly into a general acceptance of Standard German German in all three countries, as the

> trained standard speaker [from Germany] was accepted, by all respondents, whether from Germany, Austria or Switzerland, as "pure Hochdeutsch".
>
> (Herrgen 2015: 155)

I argue that there is no surprise at all that German German carries the most prestige in some categories, especially as the term "Hochdeutsch" is inextricably linked with German German in both Austria and Switzerland. In the same book, Peter (2015: 144), for instance, agrees "that the Federal German standard variety generally carries the greatest prestige", yet he does not fail to add that

> this result does however not allow the conclusion that the speakers beyond Germany would also generally follow in their standard language production the norm of the Federal Republic.
>
> (Peter 2015: 144)

This result is no surprise on some domains such as prestige (see below), if we consider the notion of linguistic insecurity (which is unknown to many dominant variety speakers). If Austrians are asked to rank speakers between

"reines Hochdeutsch"—"pure Hochdeutsch" and "tiefster Dialekt"—
"deepest dialect" (Herrgen 2015: 157), the respondents will inevitably rank
the German speakers "better"—as "Hochdeutsch" is, in Austrian perception, what Germans speak. While the use of this German-biased term ren-
ders the entire data questionable, Herrgen boldly concludes:

> The target norm "spoken standard language" is obviously identical
> with the concept of "Federal German Standard" in the three countries
> in comparison. Remarkable is also that, secondly, the assessment of
> the sample S-A., i.e. the standard of trained speakers from Austria. The
> respondents from Austria (in contrast to those from Germany and Swit-
> zerland) accept this sample as much as the federal German sample as
> "pure Hochdeutsch". In other words: two standards obviously exist in
> Austria, which are equally accepted: an Austrian and a Federal German
> standard.
>
> (Herrgen 2015: 155)

It is striking that Herrgen does not mention the factor of linguistic insecurity, which would go a long way towards explaining the detected prestige of
Standard German German in Austria in certain official contexts and the air
of "authority" and "distance" that comes with it. Dürscheid (2009: 60), for
instance, shows that most German speakers would view one kind of "Hochdeutsch" as more correct than other national varieties, which is an expression of linguistic insecurity. Linguistic insecurity is an aspect that German
mother tongue instruction in Austria and Switzerland has not successfully
managed to address and allay.

More relevant than the results for pure *Hochdeutsch* would have been to
see the results for "intelligible standard", "clear standard" or even "pleasant
standard", or another unambiguous term. If one is interested in subjective
assessment—perception—one should use terms that speakers in all locations can interpret in unbiased ways. "Hochdeutsch" is no such term (e.g.
Preston 1998; Jenkins 2007; Babel 2010).[1]

In Canadian English, for instance, a similar result can be seen in comparison with English English and American English. A socially balanced sample of Vancouverites (14–80+, gender and ethnicity diversified, n = 429),
unlike Herrgen's students, rates English English as the "best" and "most
correct" English, but they do not accept English English as a standard in
their country and see it as foreign (Dollinger 2019b: table 4.5). The conclusion that two equally accepted standards exist in Austria is quite ludicrous
from a speaker-based point of view: if people use Standard German German in Austria, they are always and inevitably first marked as outsiders,
as someone from Germany (speakers socialized in Germany are generally
immediately identifiable within a few syllables, which includes distinct

suprasegmental prosodic patterns that are easily be picked up; see Muhr's 2007 contrastive Aut-Ger pronunciation database).

In disregard of this literature, Herrgen goes even further by announcing a new "era" in German dialectology of an "Entnationalisierung" ("de-nationalization") of the standard in German. An agent for this change is quickly found:

> Since about 1990, before the de-nationalization of the mass media and with it the de-nationalization of the phonetic realizations of national standard varieties.
>
> (Herrgen 2015: 157)

If media liberalization could so easily revert a national standard, such a standard would not have been worth much. Contrary to Herrgen's claim, German TV channels broadcasting in Austria (Pro7, RTL etc.) often use Austrian commercial windows, which run spots in Austrian Standard German rather than German German. If there were no commercial need for it, TV companies would surely not spend money on new productions and/or dubbing, but just run their German German ads unchanged.

What is noteworthy is that Herrgen uses Muhr's (2003) findings on German-dominated TV but arrives at very different conclusions. Herrgen claims that Standard Austrian German is pushed back as a sign of modernity that is expressed by Standard German German. Muhr, however, speaks of the

> factors which contribute to the ongoing process of language shift [. . .]: the relative powerlessness of a small language culture [Austria] in permanent contact with a powerful one [Germany], the prestige of new media and their associated language usages which frequently symbolise modernity and worldliness, and lack of linguistic pride [in Austria], such that the native variety is considered outmoded and provincial.
>
> (Muhr 2003: 103)

Is the result of the haplessness of Austrian linguists and teachers now linguistic modernity or still linguistic imperialism? Muhr suggests that the current situation in Austria warrants language planning measures to prevent the further influence of an exonormative standard in Austria, by which, he does not envisage a restrictive body such as the *Académie française*. Herrgen, by contrast, seems to be happy with an exonormative perspective.

The conclusion of two equally eligible standards in Austria disregards evidence that a Standard German German is perceived as exonormative, or foreign, in Austria. A recent anecdote from an Austrian daily newspaper illustrates the general point: Martin Harnik, Austrian national team football player who grew up in Hamburg, is a speaker of Standard German German.

He, like his Swiss-raised national team mate Moritz Bauer, reports being labelled outsiders within the Austrian National Football team. While Bauer speaks Swiss and Harnik speaks German German, Harnik notes that Bauer "definitely did not have as difficult as time as me",[2] which illustrates the point that hailing from the dominant country (Germany) may trigger more pronounced reactions than coming from smaller countries (Switzerland).

Herrgen's study is tendentious (as is my above anecdote) as it looks at Austria and Switzerland through a German lens. It places a lot of weight on a minuscule difference in the form of the German standard speaker scoring slightly better than the Austrian standard speaker. Given the historical and sociolinguistic situation and long-standing attempts by the Duden Verlag to promote Standard German German as a monocentric standard, it is no surprise that the German Standard carries some forms of prestige. This fact has been known in German linguistics, such as in Peter's (2015) socially sensitive, fine-tuned and balanced reasoning published in the same collection as Herrgen's text, raising also the question of editorship that would normally notice obvious contradictions.

7.2.2 Methodological Problems

The study that leads Herrgen to conclude that national varieties are a thing of the past is a perceptual study with university students in Marburg, Germany, Vienna (Wien), Austria and Fribourg (Freiburg), Switzerland. Students in Germany, Austria and Switzerland listened to audio samples via loudspeaker in lecture halls from national news anchors, less formal standard speakers and traditional dialect speakers and were then asked to fill in a paper questionnaire.

A serious problem in Herrgen's study are the terms used in connection with the 7-tiered semantic differential scales in between "reines Hochdeutsch" (pure Hochdeutsch) and "tiefster Dialekt" (deepest dialect). As the term "Hochdeutsch" is biased and in Austria associated with northern Germany, these terms are not adequate to measure speaker loyalties towards Standard Austrian and Standard Swiss German. In addition, "tiefster Dialekt" is a loaded term as well, the kind that should be avoided with range scales in written questionnaires. As both ends of the scale are suboptimal, the elicited data needs to be questioned for its overall validity (Dörnyei 2003; Dollinger 2015a: 238–239).

There are further methodological issues. On the questionnaires that students were asked to fill out, the logos for Marburg University and the "Deutscher Sprachatlas" are displayed (Herrgen 2015: 157). Because "Deutscher" as well as Marburg is or can be read as referring to Deutschland, not Austria or Switzerland, these names act as indirect cues that favour German and not Austrian variants, signalling a desired benchmark. In settings in which linguistic insecurity is a factor, such obvious markers of the dominant variety need to be avoided. No mitigation is documented against these kinds of observer's paradoxes that speakers of the non-dominant standard varieties are routinely confronted with (see Dollinger 2015a: 252–268 for some strategies).

Another problem relates to group sampling. By asking university students, largely in the age cohort of 18–25, the study exclusively polls speakers of Austrian German who have seen more exposure to German norms. If students in German Studies programs were polled, a field that is now considerably influenced by pluri-arealists, they will have been exposed to monocentric lines of thought. For others, it is reasonable to assume that at least some preferences for German German are age-graded changes, changes that will be reduced or reversed once these individuals reach active work life (see Chambers & Trudgill's 1998: 78–79 for cases in Norwich, England). There is evidence for age grading in Austrian German, as the idea of the "Germanization" of Standard Austrian German has been a main trope since the early twentieth century, as we've seen in Wittgenstein (1926) and, more recently, in the new pluri-areal lore.

In any case, the negligibly higher acceptance rates for German German than Austrian German in Herrgen's study can also be explained by a volatility that would manifest itself in linguistically more conservative and thus more prestige-laden answers, or answers that are assumed to please the experimenter. We are not informed who went into the lecture halls to administer the surveys. Any German German accents, intonation and lexical or grammatical choices of the experimenters would further skew in favour of German German.

Beyond these problems, there is a more general point that should be considered. While a news anchor's speech is one way to model standard linguistic behaviour, in the Austrian case it is not necessarily the best one. As Moosmüller (1991; Moosmüller, Schmid and Brandstätter 2015) points out, better representatives of Standard Austrian German are educated Austrian speakers, as with news anchors, pronunciation norm guidelines have traditionally been somewhat influenced by Standard German German.

In any case, Herrgen's study needs to be seriously questioned. It would require re-analysing in the light of the points brought forth here and, ideally, replication with the methodological problems addressed. Until then, we should not accept the "de-nationalization" thesis. Even with the current data, the "denationalization" claim is not supported and is an artefact of an anti-pluricentric, monocentric view.

7.3 German Mother Tongue Instruction

Austrian German as the language of education has been the subject of a project by de Cilia and Ransmayr.[3] It offers important in-depth data about

Austrian high-school students, their teachers and their attitudes towards German in the Austrian context. We have seen in Chapter 3 that Teacher Dutch is an established category in the Belgian context, a category that has not been extensively studied in Austria. In the light of "low scales of loyalty towards local variants" (Schmidlin 2011: 299) in German, attitudinal data on teachers and students promises to uncover reasons for lower loyalties and to help answer the question what it is that teachers do *not* teach the Austrian and Swiss students.

From Canadian research, we know of linguistic insecurity in comparison with the dominant varieties of American or British English. This insecurity results in British English, actually English English, being ranked as "the best" English, with Canadian English in second place and American English in third (Dollinger 2011). British English has not always been the "best" variety. In the late 1970s, for instance, American English used to rank higher than Canadian English (Warkentyne 1983). In the Canadian context, however, no one would seriously suggest that Standard American English is an equally accepted standard in Canada today, as Herrgen concluded for German German in Austria.

As to the question of what Austrian high-school teachers associate with the term "Austrian German", the answers are interesting. About 61% of university-educated teachers consider *Austrian German* the variety of TV and radio newsreaders, therefore *Standard Austrian German*, while those who attended an educational college do so in only 33%. In short, the higher the education, the greater the awareness of an Austrian standard variety. Likewise, in Canadian English, a considerably higher awareness of Canadian English can be attested in the better educated, which would suggest that the teaching of Austrian German is a key factor in establishing the notion.

Juxtaposing the project's detailed attitude data with Herrgen's study, we can see drastic differences between the treatment of Standard Austrian German and Standard German German. Figure 7.2 illustrates Austrians' associations with the Austrian (diamonds) and the German standard (squares) for a number of attributes. As in Herrgen's data, Standard German German is considered as marginally more *correct, educated, fast* and *direct*, which is, given the linguistic insecurity, no surprise. On the other hand and in stark contrast to Herrgen (2015), Austrian Standard German fares considerably better in all other nine categories: Standard Austrian German is (much) more *likeable, melodious, soft, pleasant, familiar, neutral, beautiful, polite* and *comfortable* and more *indirect* than Standard German German.

It is clear that the two standard varieties are anything but "equally" accepted in Austria. More than one full point difference is assigned for a "more beautiful" Austrian standard. Herrgen's interpretation of two equally accepted standards in Austria might be taken as indicative of the goal of the pluri-areal paradigm, as the idea of a "dual standard" was uncritically

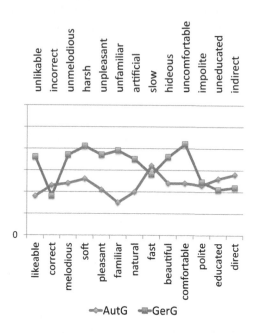

Figure 7.2 Attitudes of Austrian teachers towards Standard Austrian German and Standard German German

Source: after Ransmayr (2016)

reported in Koppensteiner and Lenz (2016) as a baseline (changed in Koppensteiner & Lenz 2017).

One of the most relevant findings in de Cillia and Ransmayr (forthcoming) is the result of an indirect polling of the status of the German language standards. Their findings are based on socially sensitive questions and contexts, being aware of the unfamiliarity of Austrians, even teachers, with linguistic terminology and of the dangers of linguistic insecurity. High-school teachers and students were asked the following question (translated from German):

> How do you consider the German language? Please tick where appropriate.
> I consider German as
>
> - a uniform language with a single standard (Hochdeutsch) form, which applies to all German-speaking countries.
> - a language with differences in the standard language (in Hochdeutsch) among the countries.

As Figure 7.3 shows, nearly 90% of Austrian high-school teachers believe that German is a language with more than one standard, as do 79% of Austrian high-school students. As awareness is a question of education, we can see why the teachers may score higher than their students. In Canada, the picture is analogous: 84% of Canadians in Vancouver with a four-year university degree believe in a "Canadian way of speaking", while just 73% without such education see Canadian identity expressed in Canadian English (Dollinger 2019b: table 4.5).

Judging by sociolinguistic principles, such data documents a need to develop teaching techniques and materials that are sensitive to Austrian German in schools. It clearly shows that the "pluri-areal" construct is against the perceptions of the speakers of German in Austria, of whom more than 4 in 5 "believe" in an "Austrian Standard German (Hochdeutsch)", as de Cillia, Fink and Ransmayr (2017: Abb. 3) show. Knowledge of internal variation in German, of norms, of processes how standards are created, would allow Austrian children and adolescents, who often grow up speaking an Austrian dialect and need to acquire, usually without educational support, Standard Austrian German, important insights into their linguistic socialization. If these students are offered lessons in German class on Austrian German, they would be better equipped for the task and, importantly, they would feel better about their varieties—because they have an Austrian "roof" to conceptualize their varieties under. As most Austrians are, in contrast to the situation in Germany on the whole (see the Marburg student response in Figure 7.1), bi-dialectal speakers of German, an awareness and

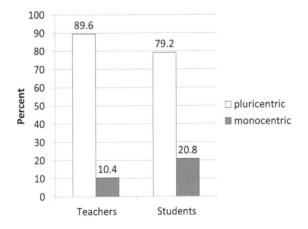

Figure 7.3 Perceptions of German in Austria

Source: de Cillia (2016); see de Cillia, Fink and Ransmayr (2017: Abb. 2)

active teaching of Standard Austrian German would help in their linguistic development.

7.4 Language Planning and Pedagogy

The last major steps in the standardization of European languages in the late nineteenth and early twentieth centuries were top-down, mandated processes. Today such approaches would not work, as we require more subtle, nuanced and ultimately democratic processes for the shaping and adaptation of our existing standards. It goes without saying that some top-down body, such as the Orthographic Conference for German, whose last reform stems from 1996, is not the way to go.

Codification should be a much more democratic and inclusive process than a century ago. Those who engage in codification need to pay attention to the speakers' identities, however complex and vulnerable they might be. The case of First Nations lexicography teaches us the basic principles. Whenever a dictionary or a grammar of a First Nations (or Native American) language is being prepared, which are often languages with only a few active speakers left, we can see very clearly a principle that should be adopted in a form that is suitable to the more widely used languages. In First Nations lexicography, the community is asked and involved at every step of the way: it is their language. While they are the guardians, they do not have the linguistic and lexicographical expertise to decide on questions such as spelling and phonetization or the consideration of variation. In this process, the principle is applied "that a speaker's or writer's linguistic identity should not be obliterated in the standardization process" (Rice & Saxon 2002: 137–138).

While the situation of Austrian German speakers is not comparable to the communities of the Dogrib (some 2000 speakers), Lekwungen (a sleeping language with currently no native speakers) or Musqueam speakers (currently revived with dozens of second-language speakers)—three languages in the Canadian west—the general principle must hold in the cases of Belgian Dutch, Austrian German, Luxembourgish, Swedish and Norwegian: the speakers and writers need to find themselves as much as possible in the standard variety.

This is the point at which language pedagogy comes into play. There has been discontent among teachers of German as a Second Language (GSL) as teaching materials do not adequately reflect the (national) varieties of German. These materials, whether textbooks, dictionaries or learner grammars, are heavily based on a Standard German German, which triggers considerable problems when used in Austria or Switzerland. It is therefore of no surprise that the GSL community has been advocating to better reflect national variation in German. Scanavino's (2015) study of labelling practices finds

Germanisms in dictionaries claiming to represent the German-speaking countries. He concludes with the insight that

> users from Switzerland and Austria have problems recognizing the lexical standard variants in their countries, because German German terms (Germanisms) are not marked as such.
>
> (Scanavino 2015: 9)

The sociohistorical deconstruction of the dominance of the German German variety would go some way towards the linguistically equal treatment of speakers. The Duden dictionaries are a case in point. While they are presented as "covering the entire German-speaking area", they are heavily based on Germany's forms and norms. When the ÖWB is criticized for not clearly labelling particular terms for their formality (standard, nonstandard), regional provenance (A, D, CH or subareas or greater regions), the critique is lopsided, because some people expected

> from the dictionary [ÖWB] a greater degree of authority, which the Duden volumes themselves are lacking.
>
> (Ammon 1995: 366)

I would add that the professional critique against the ÖWB, but the acceptance of Duden, is an expression of a double standard in German Studies, where German German is frequently considered as more correct than Austrian or Swiss.

7.4.1 The Austrian Merger in Long [e:]

The problem of unmarked German German forms—forms that are largely limited to (parts of) Germany but are presented as universal—is not limited to lexis. In my first year teaching GSL in Vienna, I was confronted in lesson 2 of a popular GSL textbook with a phonetic distinction that was irrelevant for the Austrian context. The distinction in the middle vowel in *Käse* ("cheese") with a long open [ɛː] and *Beet* ("(flower) bed") with a long closed [eː] is one that is near categorically lost in Austria; it's an older norm that no longer occurs in Austria but that is still used in most varieties in Germany. If Austrian speakers of German apply the open [ɛː], the speaker is marked as either German, ultra-conservative, posh, perhaps joking or is trying to indicate spelling with an umlaut <ä>.

Hobel, Moosmüller and Kaseß (2016) have shown that this phonetic change from the originally open long [ɛː] to the closed [eː] has reached a near categorical degree in Austria. In my interpretation, we can speak of Austrian German as having a different phonetic system today than German

German in that regard: as a system that has lost the [ɛ:]. As pluricentricity theory predicts, Standard Austrian German has developed an idiosyncratic phonological feature. As Moosmüller, Schmid and Brandstätter (2015) put it:

> Analyses of production reveal that S[tandard]A[ustrian]G[erman] is largely the outcome of a contact situation (Brandstätter & Moosmüller 2015). [Standard Austrian German] SAG stands between SGG [Standard German German] and the Middle Bavarian dialects (MBDs).
>
> (Moosmüller, Schmid & Brandstätter 2015: 340)

In Moosmüller, Schmid and Brandstätter's (2015: 343) data, long open [ɛ:] "has completely merged with /eː/". This is as predicted in the models of dialect contact (Trudgill 1986), new-dialect formation (Trudgill 2004) and the dynamic model (Schneider 2007).

While Germans seem to have begun to merge their mid-front open long vowels in a closed [e], it would be misconstruing the situation if we applied the Axiom of Categoricity against Austrian German, especially since the feature is widely noticed and has been enregistered, in my opinion, as Austrian German, much like *eh* in Canada (see Dollinger & Fee 2017: s.v. "eh"). The following examples from Canada illustrate this point that is missing pluri-areal reasoning. In any case, pedagogically speaking, it would not make sense to teach such features in a German language course in Austria, yet there it was, in lesson 2 of an A1 Beginner German course.

7.4.2 The Canadian Low-Back Vowel Merger

There is an interesting analogue to the Austrian [ɛ:]–[eː] merger in the phonological system of Canadian English. In Canada, the vowels in PATH, TRAP and LOT—all distinct in English English—have merged into one. The change has been, probably like the mid-front long-vowel merger in Austria, in progress for a few decades. Labov carried out his first study on the phenomenon in the 1960s, while the *Linguistic Atlases of the US and Canada* polled the merger since their inception in 1929. With that data, the merger was dated back to the 1880s in the two locations marked in Figure 7.4 by the heavy dotted lines in Western Pennsylvania and Eastern New England.

The low-back vowel merger is, just like the mid-front long-vowel merger in Austria, not unique to Canada, as it is used in large parts of the Western US (see Figure 7.4). The criterion of uniqueness for an identifier of a variety, as required by the "pluri-arealists", would be a benchmark that no variety fully meets.

The distinctive Canadian aspect in the low-back vowel merger is that it has become associated with Canada in expert linguist accounts, but has not been, unlike *eh*, enregistered—linguistically stereotyped—as Canadian. In

Canada the merger has been nearly categorical from about the 1930s to the present, while in the US it covers "only" half the country (the "third dialect" in the vast west, as seen in Figure 7.4). The merger did not originate in Canada; it was imported from Western Pennsylvania and Eastern New England, yet there is compelling evidence for its existence in "in the 1830s for both Nova Scotia and Ontario" (Dollinger 2010: 203).

The merger is listed as Canadian in any overview of Canadian English (e.g. Avis 1973; Brinton & Fee 2001; Chambers 2010: 20). One then needs to ask the question why the low-back merger is considered Canadian but the front-mid long-vowel merger has not been called Austrian? The situations are remarkably parallel, yet there has been hesitation to declare the phonological system of Standard Austrian German as *any* different from Standard German German.

What might be possible reasons for the differential treatment? Who would be threatened if we labelled features from an Austrian perspective? The resistance may have to do with a strict differentiation between linguistic description and language planning. As Kloss suggested, it does not matter by which sociolinguistic process varieties change, whether slowly over centuries or more quickly as an expression of social developments:

> Languages, as implied by the very concept of ausbau (reshaping), may change not merely because of those slow processes which we are prone to call natural. To a larger extent, language change is the result of innovating language planning.
>
> (Kloss 1993: 167)

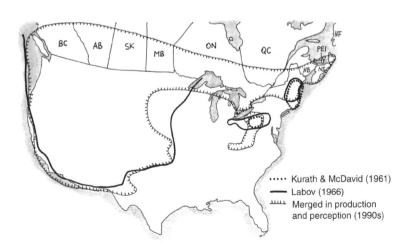

Figure 7.4 Low-back vowel merger 1930s to 1990s: spread
Source: ANAE, Map 9.4

A problem occurs when linguistic research rejects the expressed need of
language speakers, and it seems that the following attitude, once more
reported by Kloss, noticed a generation ago in "Europe", seems widespread
in Germany today:

> Innovating language planning [. . .] is a legitimate, permissible, and
> (in many cases) a necessary way of changing a language. I am not sure
> whether this sounds like a banal truism to American scholars. It cer-
> tainly is not a truism in Europe.
>
> (Kloss 1993: 167)

The versatility of the pluricentric approach has not escaped some "pluri-
arealists". Those that deal with language pedagogical questions are open to
the usefulness of pluricentricity in teaching and thus contradict their own,
more categorical statements against it in their dialectological research. Dürscheid is a good example, when she states that

> there may be reasons why the pluricentric approach is not addressed
> in German teaching. But there can be no reasons why the pluricentric
> approach should not be taught in teacher education.
>
> (Dürscheid 2009: 68)

I see in the above statement not just a contradiction with core pluri-areal
lore—why use it in pedagogy if in research pluricentricity is rejected?—but
an internal contradiction, as linguistic tolerance can only be effectively taught
if all students, in dominant and non-dominant locations alike, are exposed to
the idea of multiple standard varieties. Trudgill says the following:

> The denigration of whole groups of our fellow human beings because
> their grammatical structures or pronunciation are different from ours
> can have no more justification than the denigration of people because
> the colour of their skin is different from ours.
>
> (Trudgill 2018)

I would add that the pluri-areal denigration of Standard Austrian German
falls in the same category as the discrimination against speakers of non-
standard dialects, as it deprives people of their right to be educated in an
endonormative standard.

Notes

1 That no Austrian dialect speaker was used, Di-A, is another problem.
2 www.derstandard.at/2000063386072/Moritz-BauerIch-bin-ein-neugieriger-
   Mensch (11 Nov. 2018).
3 See http://oesterreichisches-deutsch.bildungssprache.univie.ac.at for details.

8 Examples
Trends, Not Categoricity

Languages change incrementally and in trends that rarely reach categoricity. Demanding categoricity would have "prevented" the development of a German language out of Proto West Germanic, or the split of Norwegian from Danish. This chapter discusses four variables that are profoundly Austrian, yet difficult to identify. I will compare these with examples from Canadian English to show that if there were no Austrian German, then there should also be no Canadian English, highlighting the cross-disciplinary incompatibility of the "pluri-areal" stance.

8.1 An Undetected Austrianism: *Anpatzen* ("Make Disreputable")

The lexical item *Anpatzen* (n.), which is the act of dragging one's opponent, often political opponent, into the dirt, may seem non-standard to many in Germany. In Austria, the chancellor, his opponents and the media have been using *Anpatzen* since 2017, as in the example:

> Es ist Zeit, dass Kurz mit dem Anpatzen aufhört und die Konsequenzen aus seinem schamlosen Gesetzesbruch zieht.
>
> (*Der Standard*, 7 Nov. 2018)

Using DCHP-2 methodology (Dollinger 2016c), which normalizes the biggest text collection in the world—the Google index—the results for *ein Anpatzen* are shown in Figure 8.1.

The data speak a clear language: the distribution in major Austrian news, e.g. "ein Anpatzen von seiten der SPÖ" ("an attempt of discreditation by the Austrian Socialdemocratic Party"), is Austrian Standard German on virtue of its use in quality media. The frequency index count, a comparable measure, is based on a mere seven examples in the. de domain, six of which refer to Austria, leaving one "real" German example. The use is not attested on .ch for Switzerland on both checked dates in 2018. Clearly, the diaglossic-type

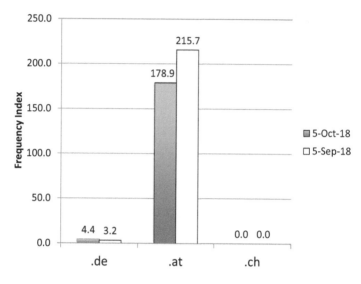

Figure 8.1 Normalized use of "ein Anpatzen"
After: Dollinger (2016c, normalizer "die")

distribution of variants (Auer's point b), is different in AutG than in GerG for that variable. If such tests are performed on a couple thousand meanings (for CanE, see Dollinger & Fee 2017, s.v. "Introduction"), the differences between Standard Austrian and Standard German German would emerge. The information in the ÖWB should be treated as a list to be tested against Austrian and non-Austrian data. That would be hypothesis-driven testing (we assume *ein/das Anpatzen* "making politically disreputable" is Standard Austrian German. Then, let us see if we can falsify that claim). For that testing, a typology of Austrianisms similar to the one for Canadian English (Dollinger 2015b) is presented in section 8.5.

8.2 An Unlikely Austrianism: *der Tormann* ("Goal Tender")

The soccer term *Tormann* is marked in Ammon et al. (2016: s.v. "Tormann") as "A, D", so used in Austria and German. *Torwart* is also marked "A, D", while *Goalie* is marked as "A, CH". *Torhüter*, in addition, is marked as "common German" (*gemeindeutsch*), that is, the unmarked variety. Ammon et al. (2016) use sample texts deemed as standard in the respective countries and a team of expert judges marking "strange" terms. In Figure 8.2, the DCHP-2 method was used to see whether the existing picture could be

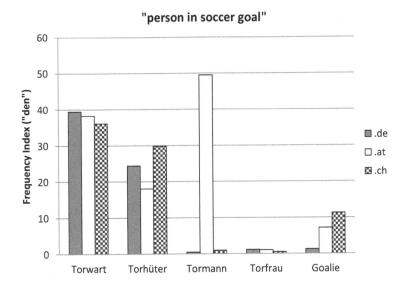

Figure 8.2 Tormann in .de, .at and .ch domains

refined. We notice that *Torhüter* is not nearly as commonly used throughout the DACH countries and that *Torwart* is slightly more frequent than *Torhüter*. While *Goalie* is a more minor form in Austria and Switzerland, reflecting the Ammon et al.'s (2016) finding, what is remarkable and not noted is that *Tormann* clearly stands out as an Austrian form, with German and Swiss uses being negligible.

With these data, we can see how even a profoundly pluricentric work may miss particular Austrian terms whose discourse frequency is higher in Austria. I use *Tormann* as an example of national variants that have not yet been detected and that await exploration, for which big data methods would need to be employed. In light of the unexpected Austrian dimension of *Tormann*, Peter Handke's 1970 novel *Die Angst des Tormanns beim Elfmeter* (in 1972 translated by Michael Roloff with the verbatim title translation *The Goalie's Anxiety at the Penalty Kick*) acquires a new Austrian reading in the title, a dimension that has remained probably undetected. What "pluri-arealists" need to realize is that they ought to stop counting types: asking if *Tormann* is known/used in Germany is too imprecise; how is it used and by whom would require other techniques.

8.3 An Even Unlikelier Austrianism: *hudeln*

The next item is an even unlikelier candidate for specifically Austrian German usage than *Tormann*, considering that the verb *hudeln* is of old

Germanic stock. I'm not aware of anyone having studied the variable contexts of the word. My attention was first drawn to it when I heard a newsreader in Austrian flagship quality radio news, *Ö1 Mittagsjournal*, which many say it is the best newscast in Austria, use the past participle *gehudelt* when reporting on a politician's hasty actions. A domain search like in Figure 8.2 above produced tens of thousands of hits across all three top-level domains and was not particularly revealing, as too many different functions of *gehudelt* were lumped together by the search. It seemed likely, however, that stylistically *hudeln* is used in more formal registers and text types in Austria than elsewhere, which formed a working hypothesis for falsification.

The question was how to test that *hudeln* may count as a standard form in Austria. There were some signs in the traditionally conservative Duden dictionaries that *hudeln* has more formal character in Austria: "Usage: Austrian colloquial, otherwise rural colloquial".[1] Another obvious contender was quality print media. Schmidlin has shown based on the *Variantenwörterbuch* data that there are marked differences between Austrian and Swiss quality papers on the one hand—the non-dominant varieties—and German quality papers on the other hand:

> Overall it needs to be noted that the middle-quality to high-quality newspapers show varying degrees of national variants. The high number of national variants in Austrian high-quality newspapers and in middle-quality papers in Switzerland is remarkable.
>
> (Schmidlin 2011: 162)

Scholars agree that the forms used in the Austrian mass media are a good indicator for the Austrian standard (Ransmayr 2018: 170), often better than books, which are often geared towards the German market—though, as the example of *Tormann* has shown, some non-German diction escapes even the copy editor.

Figure 8.3 shows the data for three German quality dailies, the *Frankfurter Allgemeine Zeitung*, the Hamburg *Abendblatt* and the Munich *Süddeutsche Zeitung*; the latter will be particularly interesting for its Bavarian provenance in relation to the Austrian quality newspapers *Die Presse* and *Der Standard*. Most interestingly in Figure 8.3, the Swiss papers, *Neue Zürcher Zeitung* (Zurich) and *Berner Zeitung* (Berne), do not show any tokens of *gehudelt*.

On the left-hand side of the figure, one can see *gehudelt* in the German papers, which is not used nearly as frequently as in the Austrian quality dailies. This is where pluri-areal interpretations would stop, claiming that there was nothing special about *hudeln*. It is where pluricentric linguists get started. Corpus linguists and sociolinguists will note, for instance, that

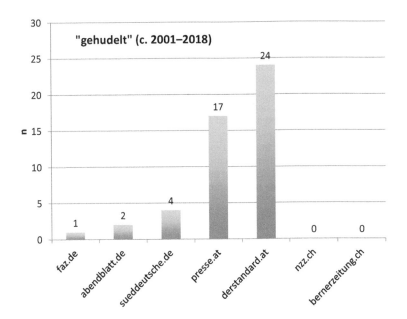

Figure 8.3 gehudelt in DACH quality print media

for mid-to-lower frequency tokens like *hudeln*, a differential of 41 tokens in AUT vs. 7 in GER (4 of which in Bavaria) should not be brushed aside. Such evidence alone would suffice to propose that *hudeln* has higher discourse frequencies in Austria, at least in the more formal written registers.

Further analysis of these examples indeed suggests a different functional range of *hudeln* in Austria. Like other terms that are considered old-fashioned in Germany but are current in Austria, e.g. *Gewand* ("Kleidung"), *Jänner* ("Januar"), *tummeln* ("sich beeilen"), *gehudelt* has much greater versatility in Austria. While *hudeln* is coded for [+DATED], [+INFORMAL] or [+RURAL] in Germany, no such connotations seem to exist in Austria, where it seems to be [+STANDARD]. Such differences in use, of course, require education. When an Austrian says *Gewand* and is laughed at by German friends, it would need to be known that it is the Germans' ignorance because Austrian German is in that respect more traditional.

When we look at the four uses of the past participle on sueddeutsche.de (four in the past 20 years), one can see that *hudeln* is used in a proverbial sense. Three of the four examples show a generic referent, two of which (2014 and 2008) are clearly proverbial constructions, and all four examples occur in the agentless passive, *wird + nicht + gehudelt*.

Table 8.1 gehudelt on sueddeutsche.de (5 Oct. 2018)

2015	Und die Entwicklung neuer Motoren braucht nun mal genugend Zeit, was passiert, **wenn gehudelt wird**, zeigt der aktuelle VW-Skandal.	specific
2015	Wer geht schon gerne auf Empfänge? Endlose Reden in schlechter Luft, während draußen der Prosecco warm wird, **gehudelt wird beim Lob**, aber nicht beim Ablaut, weshalb alles ewig dauert, und schaut der Reporter hinterher auf seinen Notizblock, so findet er selten Berichtenswertes, sondern eher die schwierige Aufgabe, aus einer mehrstundigen und mehrstimmigen Eloge eine Essenz zu destillieren.	generic
2014	All diese Produktionen haben etwas gemeinsam. Sie wurden vom Team Madel/Feldhusen mit übergroßer Liebe zum Detail geprägt. **Da wurde nicht gehudelt**, da wurde das Medium sehr, sehr ernst genommen.	generic
2008	. . . Essen, da wird ausgiebig geratscht, **da wird nicht grehudeft**. Da nimmt man sich Zeit für Gemütlichkeit.	generic

The uses of *hudeln* are rather different on derstandard.de and diepresse.com. There, *gehudelt* is very much used in the active voice, with a specific situation and referent and with mental or material verbs, such as *hören* (2018), *wirken* (2017) or *haben* (2013) and in 2011 with the *Hudler* being named.

This corpus and discourse analysis suggests that *hudeln*-AUT and *hudeln*-GER are *not* the same. While in Germany *hudeln* is restricted in quality media as a form that is only used in lexicalized, near-fossilized constructions, in Austria *hudeln* is still a productive verb, entering apparently new combinations and, as the frequencies in print and its recent use in prestigious radio news suggests, it is a term of Standard Austrian German. We can summarize *hudeln*'s use in DACH quality media in Table 8.3.

Similar statements could be easily made about Austrian German *Pickerl* ("Aufkleber"), *Anrainer* ("Anwohner") or *abgängig* ("vermisst") (*jemand is abgängig—"someone is missing"*), all of which are part of Standard Austrian German.

Would speakers from Germany hear *hudeln* and consider it as a nonstandard dialect out of ignorance of the Austrian situation? Most likely so. Nothing, however, could be further from the term's range and versatility of use, as I aimed to show. The Duden, as we have seen, gives the users, once more, no indication of standardness in Austria, treating it as "rural colloquial" for Germany and Switzerland, and as colloquial but not Standard in Austria. The *Österreichisches Wörterbuch* (42nd ed. 2012), by contrast, does not mark *hudeln*, which means that it is considered a Standard term in Austria. The ÖWB is in this respect more precise than the Duden. As

Table 8.2 Sample for *gehudelt* from derstandard.at (5 Oct. 2018)

2018	Nur zwei Drei-Tage-Sessions im Studio waren schlussendlich notwendig, urn When I Take Your Hand einzuspielen. Das Ergebnis **hört** sich alles andere als **gehudelt an**, wartet im Gegenteil mit raffinierten Sounds zwischen Rock-RifFs und Luftigem Pup auf.	specific
2017	Und doch, insgesamt **wirkte** diese Staffel [Game of Thrones] leicht **gehudelt** und auf Fanservice bedacht.	specific
2016	Den einen hat die Sitzordnung im Saal der orthodoxen Akademie in Chania nicht gepasst. Andere fanden, es **wurde** bei den Themen des Konzils wie der Ehe oder den Beziehungen der orthodoxen Kirche zum Rest der christlichen Welt doch etwas **gehudelt**.	specific (orthodox bishops)
2013	"Ich bin mein eigenes Tempo gegangen, und **habe nicht 'gehudelt'**. Dann hat's mich plötzlich nach vorne geschwappt", freute er sich über seine Aufholjagd.	specific, direct speech (skier)
2012	Hier **wurde** weder **gehudelt** noch geschlampt. Die Liebe der Entwickler für das Spiel iiegt erkennbar im Detail.	specific (game programmers)
2011	Bugs wie schwebende Panzer oder unsichtbare Löchern im Boden gehören zum Alltag und überlastete Server sowie ein zwingendes Update zum Verkaufsstart sind Zeichen dafür, dass da doch etwas **gehudelt wurde**.	specific (game programmers)
2011	Was diesmal schiefging? **Kindel hat gehudelt**. Aber er ist ein Profi: Beim nächsten Mal wird das nicht passieren.	specific (person, media manager Kindel)
2009	hier wird wieder einmal parlamentarisch **gehudelt** und gepfuscht, dass es eine Schande isL Und am 8. Oktober müsste dann noch der Bundesrat alledem zustimmen, was einigermaßen kompliziert werden könnte—aber so weit denkt dieser Tage ohnedies kein Politiker.	specific (legislation)
2008	STANDARD: Die SPÖ hat der vorherigen Regierung eine Speed-kills-Politik vorgeworfen, jetzt peitscht auch die rot-schwarze Koalition Gesetze durchs Parlament und verzichtet etwa beim Asylgerichtshof uberhaupt auf eine Begutachtung. Warum **wird** da so **gehudelt**? Ist es das schlechte Gewissen uder eine schlechte Vorbereitung?	specific (legislation), direct speech (interviewer)

Schrodt (1997: 35) remarked a while back in what is an under-appreciated key paper on Austrian German: the "identification of Austrian German" features "cannot be argued for on the basis of discrete grammatical features, lexical functions or areal distribution patterns" because "the dynamics" of

Table 8.3 *hudeln* in German-language quality newspapers

D	***hudeln* is in use but marked as [+DATED], [+INFORMAL] or [+RURAL]**
A	***hudeln* is in use and [+STANDARD]**
CH	***hudeln* is [nearly] not in use and if it is, used like in D**

linguistic adaptation is rooted "in the precise conditions of use in actualized communication", which is considered in the case of *hudeln*; in the pluri-areal data, however, such contextualization is usually missing. A full analysis of the 1,245 tokens of *hudeln* in the *Austrian Media Corpus* (Ransmayr 2018) in comparison to relevant sections in the *German Reference Corpus* would fully settle the issue and reveal further insights on functions and uses.

Canadian Tap not Faucet: "pluri-arealists" Negate Canadian English?

In Canadian English, most identified variables are shared in one way or another, either with the USA (often) or with Britain (somewhat less often) or both (most often). The valve that regulates water flow in a sink, for instance, is called *tap* by about 80% of Canadians, which means that 20% use the term marked as American, *faucet*. Is *tap* because of that not Canadian, as the "pluri-arealists" would have it? On the contrary, Chambers assigns *tap* identity-forming functions, despite in some regions *tap* going as low as about 70%. Chambers writes:

> *tap* is one of a handful of shibboleths that distinguish Canadian English from varieties in the United States.
>
> (Chambers 2008: 12)

That Chambers' claim is reasonable shows in the benchmark of 70%, which can even be lowered further. *Running shoe*, for instance, occurs in two forms, *running shoe* and *runners*, which taken together—not individually—are used from the Province of Quebec (QC) to British Columbia (BC), see Figure 8.4, as the majority Canadian variant. In some regions (Quebec's Eastern Townships), however, the two forms rank at just over 50%, as Figure 8.4 makes clear.

In Atlantic Canada, which is comprised of the provinces of Newfoundland, Nova Scotia, Prince Edward Island and New Brunswick, only the latter of which is shown in Figure 8.4, the American form *sneakers* is the overwhelming variant and *runners/running shoe* is a small minority form.

With this example we have a near-analogous case to the often-heard point that the presence of Alemannic dialects in Austria, in the province of

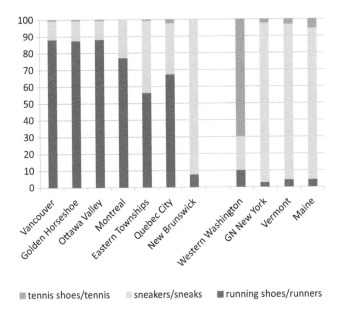

Figure 8.4 "Athletic shoe" in seven Canadian and four American regions (%)
Source: adapted from Berger (2005: Fig. 55).

Vorarlberg, forestalls the independence of Austrian German, because the state boundaries do not align with the old dialect zones. In the Canadian context, no such argument is being voiced. On the contrary, rather than lamenting about the four of the ten provinces that use the American term in the majority, linguists focus on the indeed surprising fact that in six of ten provinces *running shoes/runners* acts as an isogloss in what has traditionally been seen as one dialect zone (Boberg 2005: 146). That *any* differences should exist is striking. As in the Austrian–German case, it's a matter of perspective. *Runners/running shoe* is considered as evidence for the independence of Canadian English, despite it not being used "in the complete state territory", as the "pluri-arealists" would say. We can conclude: if there is no Standard Austrian German because of its categoricity defects, then there is also no Standard Canadian English.

8.4 An Enregistered Austrianism: *es geht sich (nicht) aus*

Austrianisms are not limited to vocabulary or pronunciation features, but extend over the entire range of linguistic levels of description. In the realm of expressions, the very frequent and versatile *es geht sich aus* ("it'll work") vs. *es geht sich nicht aus* ("it won't work") is a particularly common and useful construction that many Austrians find is not understood abroad. Today, the construction has become somewhat of an Austrian stereotype and is openly recognized as Austrian to a degree that it is being used in Germany as an indirect reference to Austria. Figure 8.5 shows the normalized internet data (DCHP-2 method).

With almost 21 index points compared to 2.8 in Germany and 2.5 in Switzerland, the .at domain stands out for the phrase. We have empirical evidence for another Austrianism. Since 2016, however, the data has been skewed somewhat. In that year, German singer and long-time resident of Hamburg, Christiane Rösinger (from the bands *Lassie Singers* and *Britta*), named one of her songs *Es geht sich nicht aus*, which she openly acknowledged as a borrowing from Austrian German. Here is the song's chorus:

> Es geht sich nicht aus
> Es wird nicht reichen
> Damit kann man keinen Stein erweichen
> Damit kann man keinen Sieg erringen
> Damit kann man keinen Blumentopf gewinnen
>   Christiane Rösinger in *Es Geht Sich Nicht Aus* (www.golyr.de/)

The song, quoted or referred to on the .de and .ch domains, is responsible for the non-Austrian scores in Figure 8.5. The song has now popularized an Austrian expression and enregistered it in the international German-language context.

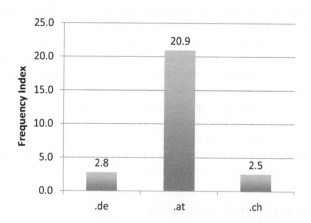

Figure 8.5 es geht sich nicht aus in .de, .at, .ch

Es geht sich nicht aus can be considered an enregistered form of Austrian German, in a similar way that *Schnitzel* is identified with Austria, or skiing, or unsuccessful soccer. We will see if and to what degree the term is picked up by non-Austrians, as it is doubtless a useful and indirect way of telling someone that an original plan/schedule/idea won't work out. It is also a good contender to form part of the Austrian standard.

8.5 A Typology of Austrianisms

We have seen in the above examples that Austrianisms come in many shapes and sizes, and a methodologically mixed toolkit that includes big data methods such as Grieve (2016) or Dollinger (2016c) is advantageous. Furthermore, the study of national varieties of German, including Austrian German, would ben-efit from a definition and typology of "–isms". Avis defined a Canadianism as

> a word, expression, or meaning which is native to Canada or which is distinctively characteristic of Canadian usage though not necessarily exclusive to Canada.
>
> (Avis 1967: xiii, qtd. from
> http://dchp.ca/dchp2/pages/how-to-use)

As a first step, we could apply his definition to an "Austrianism" as

> a word, expression, or meaning which is native to Austria or which is distinctively characteristic of Austrian usage though not necessarily exclusive to Austria.

Dollinger and Fee (2017) use six categories plus a category of non-Canadianism in their historical–comparative dictionary of Canadian English. Adapted for Austrian German, the seven types could be defined as follows.

In Type 1, obvious contenders would be food terminology, such as *Schnit-zel* and *Hascheeknödel*, the former used internationally now, the latter not so; or *Kipferl* ("croissant"); administrative terms, *Erlagschein* (though now near obsolete), *Stempelmarke* (utterly obsolete) or *Arbeitnehmerveranla-gung* ("employment tax return"); and other forms of neologisms where words were first created or first borrowed in Austrian German. The latter category would include loanwords that entered German via the Habsburg Empire, e.g. *Tollpatsch* ("clumsy person") < Hungarian, *pomali* ("slow") from Czech or *pivo* ("beer") from Southern Slavic, with the latter two not having entered Standard Austrian German. In this class also belong terms that are carried over from different times, e.g. when the French court chan-nelled a number of terms into Austrian German that are still in wide use to

Table 8.4 Typology of Austrianisms and non-Austrianisms

Type 1 — Origin: a form and its meaning were created in what is or was Austria
Type 2 — Preservation: a form or meaning that was once widespread in German varieties, but is now preserved in Austrian German; sometimes called "retention"
Type 3 — Semantic Change: forms that have undergone semantic change in Austrian English compared to other varieties
Type 4 — Culturally Significant: forms or meanings that have been enshrined in the Austrian psyche and are widely seen as part of Austrian identity
Type 5 — Frequency: forms or meanings that are Austrian by virtue of frequency
Type 6 — Memorial: forms or meanings now widely considered to be pejorative
Non-Austrian: forms or meanings once thought to be Austrian for which evidence is lacking

Source: adapted from Dollinger and Fee (2017)

today, e.g. as spellings such as *Varieté*, the dominant form in Austria, rather than *Varietee* in Germany (Ransmayr, Mörth & Ďurčo 2017: 37), *Trottoir* besides *Gehsteig* ("sidewalk") or pronouncing *Kabarett* without final /t/ in AutG, or also *fad* ("boring") rather than "*langweilig*".

Type 2 would be the relatively large part of the vocabulary that was once more widespread but has been preserved in Austrian German. We mentioned earlier das *Gewand* (or *G'wand*) ("clothing"), which is as the common core and near-standard variant today that is likely more frequent than *Kleidung/Kleider* in Austria, the major German German variant, or demonstrative pronouns AutG *da* ("here") vs. *dort* ("there") and German German *hier* ("here") vs. *da* ("there"); the different meanings of *da* in AutG and GerG lend themselves to misunderstandings, or greetings such as *Servus*, whether the Bavarians use it or not and, from Italian, *Ciao*.

Type 3 items have undergone semantic change in Austria and would need to be more thoroughly studied, but terms such as *Sessel* ("chair"), which in German German is predominantly *Stuhl* ("chair"), or *Schlag* ("whipping cream") for *Sahne*, are contenders. More complex would be modal particle *eh*, as in *Ich hab das eh gemacht* ("I did it anyway/already/regardless"), which tends to have a much wider functional range, with possible standard uses, in Austria than in other German varieties. Type 4 would be a class of terms of socio-psychological relevance. In the Canadian context these are, among others, ice hockey and universal healthcare terms, i.e. terms that deal with the mystification of the nation. In the Austrian context, this might be skiing terms from *Abfahrt* via *Slalom* to *Super G*, political terms such as *Neutralität* or *Sozialpartnerschft*, or terms like *Gemütlichkeit* ("laid-back and easy-going-ness"), which is now actively used in Tourism Austria marketing campaigns. Type 5 would be a large class of terms, from *hudeln*, as seen above, to *der Einser* ("school grade A+") rather than *die Eins*, to the temporal and spatial *es geht sich nicht aus* and probably *Busserl* ("kiss"; quite standard) or *Pickerl* ("car decal"; almost certainly standard). Many of the Type 1 terms would also be the most frequent terms; while a Type 1 claim is more difficult to establish and sometimes hard to defend in the light of new evidence, Type 5 claims are reliably established with parallel corpora of national varieties and ad-hoc data collections, as shown in the case studies adapting the DCHP-2 method. Finally, Type 6 is the flip side of Type 4 and concerns the concepts that one does not take pride in: terms of abuse for minorities, *Tschusche* ("foreigner"; derogatory), *Briefbomber* ("letter bomber Franz Fuchs") and all the Nazi terms that were part of Austrian German, too, from *Endlösung* ("extermination of the Jews") to *Endsieg* ("final victory by Hitler"), and so on. These are the terms, meanings and expressions that are part of the dark history of the nation.

Types 4 and 6 would open up the typology to a cultural aspect that has been lacking so far in much of the discussion, while Types 1, 2, 3 and 5 are based on comparative corpus-linguistic study of language in use, a comparative corpus pragmatics in a pluricentric framework, if one will. Finally, the last type is comprised of falsified meanings and terms, which are terms shown as not being Austrian. Such findings need to be published as a corrective. In the Canadian context, the six plus one types were tested on 1348 meanings; 1104 meanings have proven a Canadian dimension, Types 1–6 in the second edition of the *Dictionary of Canadianisms on Historical Principles*.

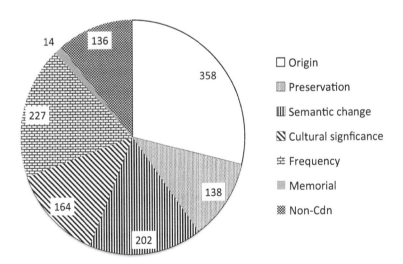

Figure 8.6 Type distribution in DCHP-2 Update

Figure 8.6 shows that almost 11% of terms that had been considered Canadian were positively falsified with our comparative method, while the other 89% are distributed unevenly among the six categories.

It stands to reason that such approach would put both the ÖWB and Duden dictionaries on a sounder empirical footing. As can be seen on www. dchp.ca/dchp2, the presence of an explicit "word story", explaining in general language why a given term is classified as Canadian, would also be most welcome in the Austrian context. The word story for the term *garburator* ("in-sink waste grinder"), for instance, is the following:

> *Type: 5. Frequency* — The term *garburator* is almost exclusively found in Canada (see Chart 1), though the US terms *garbage disposal* or *garbage disposer* are also in use (see Video).
>
> The appliance was invented in 1927 by John W. Hammes in Racine, Wisconsin, and made available in 1938 as InSinkErator (R) (DiFulco 2007, see Image 2). Though an American invention, the dominant Canadian term is *garburator*, which is virtually unknown in the US.
>
> See also COD-2, s.v. "garburator", which is marked "Cdn.", OED-3, which labels it "Chiefly Canad.".

Such discussion would be needed for each and every term and meaning in Austrian German and would take time, but with digital sources, starting with the *Austrian Media Corpus* (Ransmayr, Mörth & Ďurčo 2017), and data harvesting methods it is possible to test tens of thousands of terms for their Austrian dimensions. Lists of potential candidates exist and look promising. Schrodt's (1997: 29–34) collection, gleaned from Theodor Kramer's poems, offer plenty of material for Austrian Umgangssprache and Standard: from *ein Alzerl* ("a little bit") and *Fisolen* ("green beans"), via *Lauser* ("rascal"), *Pritsche* ("wooden cargo area") and *Spagat* ("twine") to *verkutzen* ("to splutter"), *Zipferl* ("penis") or *Zuckerl* ("candy piece"), these suspected Austrianisms as "raw material" (ibid.: 29) still await empirical, context-dependent falsification.

Note

1 "Gebrauch: österreichisch umgangssprachlich, sonst landschaftlich umgangssprachlich" (www.duden.de/rechtschreibung/hudeln, 3 Oct. 2018).

9 Safeguards in the Modelling of Standard Varieties

Ronald Pohl: Do you share with the Austrians the preference to express yourself "imprecisely"?
Herbert Grönemeyer: What you characterize as "imprecise" is the joy of the Austrians to use language smoothly. In Germany and especially in Prussia we consider language as a representative of our engineering.—We use language with great precision, but do not tend to use its playful characteristics.[1]

There should no longer be any confusion about the usefulness of pluricentricity and the emptiness of "pluri-areality", an anti-theoretical term that is synonymous with geographical variation. If we treat the Canadian–US border, the Norwegian–Swedish border or the Luxembourgish–German border one way, we cannot treat the Austrian–German border any other way, unless we have compelling reasons to set it apart from the others. As shown in this book, these special reasons do not exist. Linguists should not postulate conceptual exceptions lightly, because a term that only applies to only one setting (German) is in all likelihood not a very relevant term.

If, however, we choose to work without an explicit theory, as is the case in the pluri-areal label, we should clearly say so but stick with established terms, such as *geographical variation* or *regional variation*, which are not as obtuse or misleading as "pluri-areality". There are consequences to working without an explicit theory, though. With Popper, without theory we are leaving the "game of scientific inquiry" and are doing something else.

The pluricentric approach, and the role that conceptualizations of language and identity play in it, is missing in pluri-areal work on Austrian German and, possibly, in Belgian Dutch, but not in Norwegian, Swedish, Danish, Luxembourgish and, of course, the many varieties in the English Language Complex. If Schmidt and Herrgen's textbook (2011) is any indicator, German dialectology seems to be biased in belittling existing national identification markers, a practice that flies in the face of Ammon (1995), de Cillia (1998) and Wodak et al. (2009). When Glauninger (2013: 129) suggests that "no Austrian" has a semantic problem when she reads *Blumen-kohl* and not the Austrian term *Karfiol* ("cauliflower") in Austrian super-markets, I wonder about the motivation for the suggestion, coming from a linguist, who is suggesting the locals should not be upset when locally established and widely used Austrian terms are *not* used. The European Union does not mandate that Austrian terminology be abolished; I wonder why Glauninger thinks that would be a good idea.

We've seen in Scheuringer (1990a) the dialectological manifestation of the ONE STANDARD GERMAN AXIOM that underpins pluri-areal work, gener-ally unacknowledged. Scheuringer's study is pre-Labovian and to a con-siderable degree pre-Popperian in that it considers the "one-areality" of German verified "once-and-for-all" ("endgültig verifiziert"), which leaves us with the modelling of German shown in Figure 4.2. Scheuringer's point of view coincides with the dominant German picture and imagination. His pluricentric paper on Austrian German from 1985 is not cited in the field, while Scheuringer (1990a) is the sole basis for Auer (2005), who picked up on the obviously wrong and lopsided interpretation of the Austrian–German border.

How *should*, however, political borders and standard varieties be lin-guistically modelled? The evidence in this book shows that "pluri-areality" is no replacement for the pluricentric approach. "Pluri-areality" is rooted in a naïve positivism that works with essential absolutes (e.g. Axiom of Categoricity), neglecting basic sociolinguistic concepts (e.g. indexicalzia-tion, linguistic insecurity). The recent *Handbook of Areal Linguistics*, for instance, does not address the issue of standards within a given language in a meaningful way and considers political borders as outside of its purview (van der Auwera & van Olmen 2017: 242). Anyone studying standard varieties cannot do so.

It is known today that international borders, which are usually arbi-trarily drawn, have linguistic and cultural effects. Chambers summarizes 70 years of Canada–US border findings, stating that linguistic cross-border differences

> are the overt, measurable differences, the things we can actually hear and count. But those trivial little differences add up to something much larger. Cumulatively, they amount to dialects, viewed as the integration of numerous trivial linguistic differences, but that is not the end-point. The dialect differences form one stratum that we must then put together with differences in fashion, cuisine, recreation, manners, politics, and preferences in all kinds of things. These differences may also be trivial, taken one by one, but they amount to culture. [. . .] They [the cultural differences] persist, as we have seen, whether the "fence" is a gorge or

a meandering river or just a line on the road. A line on the road, if you think about it, is nothing at all.

(Chambers forthcoming: section 4)

The situation is generalizable, including the Austrian–German, Flemish–Dutch or Luxembourgish–German contexts. One should note that in the Canadian context unspecified benchmarks for type counts are *not* used. The argument of small differences between the Austrian and German standards are particularly weak. The purported 3% in lexis, 3 in 100 words, as Austrian German may not sound much, but neither does the 2% difference between the genomes of the chimpanzee and the human. Simple bean counting will not suffice.

In any case, the linguist is not the one to decide what "counts" and what does not, as this role is always reserved for speaker collectives (see section 9.3). It is one thing that "pluri-arealists" consider Austrian differences with German German as "trivial". They may choose to do so. But it is an entirely different affair to coin and propagate a concept that enforces implicitly cultural biases about other varieties. In the following, I offer three fail-safes for standard variety modelling: the application of the "horizontal" version of the uniformitarian principle (see 9.1), the requirement to use falsifiable theories in the study of dialectology (see 9.2) and that speaker attitudes, including linguistic insecurity and power differentials are addressed (9.3). Rounded off by two sections, these principles will be discussed in turn.

9.1 The Uniformitarian Principle: "Vertical" and "Horizontal"

All variables in the previous chapter have shown some claim to Austrianness and, in most cases, also a claim to be standard. Comparing Austrian German with Canadian English, two non-dominant varieties, I apply the uniformitarian principle, which was originally developed for historical linguistics and language change (e.g. Labov 1994; the principle is at the base in Weinreich, Labov & Herzog 1968 but not mentioned by name). As I tried to show throughout this book, we must not treat cases such as Austrian German and Canadian English differently, given their striking structural parallels since 1945; the principle's expansion would prevent differential treatment.

The uniformitarian principle has been the cornerstone in historical linguistics. Introduced from geology into linguistics by William Dwight Whitney in the 1860s, the sociolinguists of the 1960s, who set out to rival historical linguistics as the prime discipline for language change, felt the need to not only discuss the principle but also to revive it. Labov considers the uniformitarian principle "so central to [his] work" (1994: 21) that he contextualizes its application at length. Put simply, the uniformitarian principle states that

> the linguistic forces which operate today and are observable around us are not unlike those which have operated in the past.
>
> (Romaine 1988: 1454)

With this principle in mind, researches may use present-day data to explain aspects of the linguistic past where such data might be lacking. In the present context of national varieties and border studies, the principle applies not only to linguistic aspects of language, but also to the social ones. Romaine continues:

> This principle is of course basic to purely linguistic reconstruction as well, but sociolinguistically speaking, it means that there is no reason for believing that language did not vary in the same patterned ways in the past as it has been observed today.
>
> (ibid.)

Aiming to exploit the parallels between the present and the past, linguistics has been harnessing the uniformitarian principle in its diachronic application, which might be called "vertical", i.e. going back in time. If the comparison of different diachronic language states with one another is considered "vertical", then the comparison of different varieties and speech communities at a given point in time, including the present, can be considered as the "horizontal" application of the uniformitarian principle.

If we accept the vertical reading, as is a given in language change studies, but not the horizontal reading, we expose the disciplines to silo-like treatment. As a result, we have terms such as "pluri-areality", which has developed in isolation from other contexts and philologies, as a kind of "wild terminological growth". Such developments should be prevented, because they threaten a basic assumption of sociolinguistics: regardless of which languages you study, you must use established terminology unless you make a reasoned, well-argued, well-documented and convincing claim for a new concept that is exposed to international critique. The latter has not happened in 25 years for "pluri-areality". On the contrary, the non-concept is proposed to be applied to "English, French, Spanish, Russian", which Elspaß, Dürscheid and Ziegler (2017: 91) consider a "desideratum".

Accepting the horizontal interpretation, we need to be wary, as indeed with the vertical interpretation, of social situations that might *not* be equivalent. In stone age societies, for instance, radically smaller group sizes where everyone knew everyone, a "society of intimates", would have given rise to different phenomena compared to larger, more mobile societies that would develop after the invention of agriculture (Trudgill 2011). Glauninger's case (2001, 2013) for a special status of German does not meet these criteria, since it exaggerates the heterogeneity of the German standard variety in the German small state structure that was linguistically, actually, as homogenous or heterogeneous as other European standard languages at that time.

There are, however, situational differences that may block the application. For instance, the role of men and women in present-day societies in Western Europe and in Arabic countries is not compatible, with limited public roles of the latter that resulted in a marked linguistic effect (Albirini 2016: 6.3.1). Such claims, however, are not tenable between Austria, Canada or Germany.

Judging by sociolinguistic practice, which has foregrounded and thrived on a comparative element (e.g. referenced language studies in, e.g. Albirini 2016; Chambers 2009; Gold & Tremblay 2006; Labov 2001, 2010), researchers have few if any hesitations to apply the uniformitarian principle horizontally to different present-day societies. They have been making such comparisons for a long time without express recourse to the uniformitarian principle. Unless there is reason to believe that social structures differ considerably in present-day societies, sociolinguistic patterns in one society should be applicable to the next one. Pluricentricity abides by the horizontal uniformitarian principle; it is based on it. "Pluri-areality" violates it.

9.2 Explicit and Falsifiable Theories

The second basic fail-safe is the strict separation of theory, or theory-derived a priori hypotheses, and data. In the case of "pluri-areality", we have an undefined term that is identical with the descriptive term "geographical variation". The introduction of new, supposedly "objective" methods cannot replace a sound theoretical backdrop. Such designs are not felicitous and are exposed to bias and circular explanations.

Pluri-areal interpretations are not derived from theory-based research; they are not tested and checked in the sense that a theoretical statement is tested against independent data. Instead, the data is simultaneously both data *and* theory, often via some mathematical operations that are in some sort of mathematical "black box". Theory, methodology and data are one and the same. The infelicitous design of that school results in the Austrian–German border as a linguistic border being called "preposterous" (Scheuringer 1990b), the ill-conceived "de-nationalization" of the standard in German (Herrgen 2015) or the concept of a "modern pluriareal language" *in opposition* to pluricentricity (Elspaß & Niehaus 2014). The proponents reject pluricentricity because some cases are claimed not to fit pluricentric theory predictions, without offering an alternative model that meets speaker realities, attitudes and perceptions. The sociolinguistic power differential between speakers of

German in Austria and Switzerland vs. Germany and the resulting linguistic insecurity (section 7.2) is no topic in their writings. Their practice violates the customary ways of letting the speakers decide how their variety is seen.

Pluri-arealist claims to objectivity are circumspect. Herrgen's call for the use of "objective" criteria in addition to subjective (speaker-oriented) seems all too convenient, while implicitly upholding the ONE STANDARD GERMAN AXIOM. These, at their core monocentric, approaches have in common that they are, de facto, linguistically imperial stances without their proponents necessarily realizing it. Is Austrian Germain an "entirely political" construct (Elspaß & Niehaus 2014)? As these pages have shown: certainly not. But Austrian German is *also* political. As nothing in our social word is utterly un-political, including, as I have shown, pluri-areal thinking (see 9.4). Without the political reality of the Republic of Austria as an independent nation, we would be dealing with pluricentricity on a less distinct level, on a level that Bavaria might have a claim to now. Do Herrgen's and Elspaß' calls for monocentrism have a political dimension? They certainly do. "Pluri-arealists" have made it clear that they consider the social dimension as secondary to linguistic criteria; a claim that needs to be disputed. How can someone be doing sociolinguistics when key aspects of the social dimension are categorically ruled out or belittled?

Haugen (1966) has shown a long time ago that ruling out the socio-political angle is not desirable or, speaking with Popper (1966 [1934]), even possible. To announce to the speakers of Austrian German, from a linguistically powerful position in Marburg, with the backing of 80 million speakers who have largely not been sensitized to colonial issues in language, that both Standard Austrian German and Standard German German are equally accepted in Austria is insensitive at best. Let the speakers of Austrian German decide for themselves, for which de Cillia and Ransmayr (forthcoming), among others, offer very clear, unambiguous answers.

The study of Austrian German, Belgian Dutch, Luxembourgish and other non-dominant varieties should build on existing work. Auer (2005), for instance, offers falsifiable hypotheses of how national varieties are shaped in connection with political borders. We've seen Auer's (2005: 28) ranking in Chapter 4 and that the Austrian–Bavarian border meets the conditions for diversification. Scheuringer's (1990a) data shows quite clearly, against his own conclusions, that the dialects differ across the border, while the more important differences in the national standard varieties and the repertoire types are realized to a greater degree, as we know from de Cillia and Ransmayr (forthcoming), Wodak et al. (2009), even pluri-areal data (such as *Kaffee* or the example on verb sequencing), or the case studies in Chapter 8.

Biased interpretations can only be prevented if theory acts as a fail-safe, theory that is adapted by bit-by-bit testing and modification to fit the data. As we have seen in the studies discussed, pluri-arealists have not gone that way, but have chosen to reject pluricentricity outright (but look at Figure 4.1 and the room in the pyramid for variation within the pluricentric model). Had they argued that pluricentricity does not model every single case and that they wish to make a contribution merely by way of descriptive terms using a model based on geographical variation alone, the pluricentricity debate would have been avoided.

9.3 "The Speaker Is Always Right": Pedagogical Implications

Canadian kindergartners learn about Terry Fox, the national hero of extraordinary character strength; they learn Canadian spelling; but they do not hear much about Canadian English as such. In the Austrian context, there is an equally powerful case to be made that in order to alleviate linguistic feelings of insecurity, which no one can wish for, up front, targeted and sustained instruction about Austrian German is needed in Austrian schools, as argued connivingly by de Cillia, Fink and Ransmayr (2017). Such lessons would be conceived from an identity-confirming, intercultural communication and peace-promoting vantage point of mutual respect and not, as some pluri-arealists assume, from a brute nationalist angle. The Canadian model of intercultural respect, while not perfect, could go a way towards that goal. There is a need for such curricula, and a need that is more pressing since de Cillia (2015: 162) has shown that people "do not grasp the conceptual differences between varieties [such as Standard Austrian and Standard German]".[2]

In Canada, I sometimes speak of the "birthright" of Canadians to learn about Canadian English (Dollinger 2011: 8). It seems to me there is an Austrian "birthright" or "socialization right", too. It is not the schools that are failing, but primarily we dialectologists and sociolinguists. A construct such as "pluri-areality" puts speakers of Austrian German at a linguistic disadvantage. If Austrian professors of German, for instance, do *not* support a pluricentric model (currently at least four of five do not), they engage by default in a language–political act of at least indirectly supporting the traditional model that treats German German as the "unmarked" form. Whether they want to or not, they take a stance. If national variants of German "are considered as equals besides areal variants of standard German" (Niehaus 2017: 64), a devaluation of non-dominant national variants has taken place that is inherent in the pluri-areal agenda.

We, the linguists, owe it to the speakers of non-dominant varieties, including Austrian German, to take them and their speech seriously. Children and adolescents who grow up bi-dialectally—a non-standard variety and, often delayed starting with the school entry, a standard variety—as applies to most settings in Austria, are often left alone to navigate the complex linguistic variation in their linguistic socialization processes. I would estimate that about 15–20% of my high-school classmates did not fully master Standard Austrian German at age 19 and were then limited to the functions of their dialectal speech in professional engineering contexts where it was not always, e.g. dealing with German suppliers, appropriate. A pluricentric approach would remedy their problem, a "pluri-areal" approach aggravate it.

Austrian–German speakers are right in their assessment, as de Cillia and Ransmayr (forthcoming) show, that standard German is not perceived as a monolithic entity, but is structured into several norms. Linguists and dialectologists need to make such results their mandate or at least tolerate them. The old Norwegian case offers good advice in this respect:

> A distinction must be made between linguistic research and linguistic normalization and guidance. The latter must build on scientific research and take its results into account, but is not in itself a purely scientific problem. It is in equal, or to greater degree a national, social or practical-pedagogic problem.
>
> (Norwegian Language Commission 1952,
> qtd. in Haugen 1966: 298)

The acceptance of the pluricentric model in German linguistics is not just a linguistic question but also a pedagogical and social one. Its adoption would alleviate a few linguistic problems in Austria with one stroke. The description of German in at least three national frameworks would maintain the general mutual intelligibility of German on the whole, while allowing identity constructions internationally. As Wodak et al. (2009: 193) found, differences between Austrian German and German German are often perceived as existent on the vernacular (Alltagssprache) and dialectal level. The promotion of Standard Austrian German, the teaching of the concept in schools, which has been so much criticized (section 5.2), would go a long way towards resolving conflicting messages about Austrian German. This would simultaneously address the persistent "schizoid characteristics" of speakers of Austrian German:

> on the one hand, the language was an essential component of Austrianness. [. . .] On the other hand, there was hardly any awareness of an independent Austrian standard variety.
>
> (Wodak et al. 2009: 193)

9.4 The Language–Political Angle of "Pluri-Areality"

It has become clear that the pluri-areal approach is not just meant to simply describe. On the contrary, the promotion of "pluri-areal" ideas has been called an issue of "central language-political relevance" (Dürscheid, Elspaß & Ziegler 2011: 136), whose findings are supposed to "assist authors of teaching materials and teachers on the basis of the new findings in their choices of grammaticality and norm decisions" (Elspaß, Engel & Niehaus 2013: 60). No self-respecting government of an independent nation, whether in a union of states or not, would accept a view that on the one hand attacks language planning measures for Standard Austrian German, while on the other hand enforces its own understanding of "good" language planning which is implicitly rooted in a model of German German (e.g. section 5.3).

Given the increasing number of studies in the pluri-areal framework, studies which have recently been supported by larger Austrian grants and are led by Austrian-funded positions in German linguistics, some might even say that the Austrian government is currently funding research that undermines a key part of Austrian identity. It is already getting very difficult to get pluricentric work accepted in a constantly increasing sea of "pluri-areal" reviewers who enforce their own ideological angle. As I have shown, "pluri-areal" is as ideological as any other approach, believing in a ONE STANDARD GERMAN AXIOM with a model that has as its only core value the negation of pluricentricity.

It is hoped that the arguments brought forth here will help to settle on a model that is open to the conceptualization of multiple standards, as shown in Figure 4.1, rather than the pluri-areal view in Figure 4.2. As a linguist, I have found the "pluri-areal approach" almost distortive in its negation of some aspects of language without stating so clearly. It is an approach that uses a mechanical view of language at its core, void of social meaning, operating with essentialist categories that are based in categoricity in order to refute any claims of linguistic autonomy of larger political bodies. These political bodies are in themselves an expression of social networks, connections and histories. Haugen dealt with such problems earlier and summarizes:

> It must be granted that linguists are not necessarily equipped to pursue language planning. Their sensitivity to linguistic nuances may be dulled by excessive preoccupation with the mechanics of language.
>
> (Haugen 1966: 297)

What is disturbing is that this mechanical, etic approach is used to contain variation in the German standards by blocking out conceptualizations of new standards. The pluri-areal theoretical and methodological shortcomings and the select application of axioms against the non-dominant variants are worrisome developments that can only instil more insecurity into Austrian pupils and students, telling them that the German German standard, as Herrgen (2015) proclaims, is equally accepted in Austria. It is beyond doubt that children growing up in Austria will benefit much more from the motto of the *Österreichisches Wörterbuch*, which considers Austrian idiosyncrasies as "not less correct, less good or less beautiful" than any other ones. It suggests a sorry state of German dialectology if this very basic principle needs to be called on.

9.5 Considering Political Borders

In the Canadian context, Bill New makes the point that some American writers, from sheer ignorance, do not perceive Canada as an independent country, a *foreign* country. In a 1995 novel by American writer Richard Ford, New isolates the following statement:

> The best all-round Americans, in my view, are Canadians. I, in fact, should think of moving there, since it has all the good qualities of the states [USA] and almost none of the bad, plus cradle-to-grave health care and a fraction of the murders we generate. An attractive retirement waits just beyond the forty-ninth parallel.
>
> (Richard Ford, *Independence Day*, qtd. in New 1998: 74)

It is clear that this writer perceives Canada as

> an *extension* of the American persona, not as something with *intrin-sic* differences that might need to be recognized, acknowledged, or accommodated—not, that is, as a centre somewhere else.
>
> (New 1998: 74)

When "pluri-arealists" stress the common historical ties of Austria and Germany over more recent and more important identity formations (e.g. Elspaß, Dürscheid & Ziegler 2017: 72), they ignore that political borders throw a wrench into linguistic systems and geographical variation, which has been widely acknowledged for years. Boberg (2000) made an important stride in that direction, and no less than William Labov was ready to concede that "the predictions of the cascade model across the U.S.-Canada border, where the political (and structural) boundary is a categorical boundary" was not confirmed (Labov 2003: 10). Accusing Boberg and Labov of nationalism would be absurd; as absurd as chastising the pluricentric approach because there are shared cross-border variants or because not all Austrian variants are used by every single Austrian speaker. Internal variation within and across state boundaries, usually brought forth as the main counter argument once the political bias route is exploited, is no problem for a pluricentric approach, as the Norwegian case explicates.

Setting unattainable benchmarks as cut-offs for any new standard is, by contrast, not sound scholarly practice. Since categoricity is what monocen-trists demand in order to accept a Standard Austrian German, they forget that such criterion is not met by any language. There would be no Standard German, no Standard Dutch, no Standard Luxembourgish or Standard Norwegian, if categoricity were the benchmark for standardness. A serious adoption of variationist and sociolinguistic principles would result in an improvement and refinement of the pluricentric approach. A few years back, I expressed this hope with a comparison of the phonetic *Atlas of North American English*:

> The phenomenon of the Canadian Vowel Shift shows clearly that linguistic isoglosses exist that have not been detectable with the traditional methods of dialectology. I am convinced, if my anecdotal observations are not utterly off, that the Bavarian–Austrian border would also show such systemic differences between the two sides of the Inn River, so to speak, because, on the whole, Austrians speak more often with other Austrians and Germans with Germans.
>
> (Dollinger 2012b: 29)

We have seen in section 4.3 that despite European integration, which is currently stalled if not worse, the situation along the Inn River still resembles a harder border in the minds of the people than meets the eye. As it seems that some of the major proponents underappreciate the specifics of non-dominant sociolinguistic contexts, such phonetic cross-border studies might convince them.

I doubt that any colleague wishes to pursue, to use Dressler's chosen diction, "German German linguistic imperialism", though the dubious, undefined term of "pluri-areality" hinges on the ONE STANDARD GERMAN AXIOM. Let us abandon once and for all "pluri-areality" in favour of the more productive, theoretically fully grounded and pedagogically meaningful concept of pluricentricity. As Michael Clyne put it a while back:

> As national varieties are markers of national identity, their downgrading on the basis of power relationships can be seen as an instrument of oppression or an indication of low national self-esteem.
>
> (Clyne 1992a: 6)

This degradation, intended or not, is the inevitable effect of a non-pluricentric view. I agree with Scheuringer (1997: 343) in one point, when he writes that "terms once introduced have a long life, even when they are erroneous". I have made my case against "pluri-areality", which is such an erroneous term; "pluri-areality" is a term that threatens the unity of cross-philological dialectology and means nothing more than simply "geographical variation". In analogical situations, we need to use the applicable terms: just like science–theoreticians (unlike moral philosophers) cannot pick and choose, or pull a fancy-sounding term out of the hat (and leave it an empty shell with lots of smoke cover). The issue of pluricentricity vs. geographical variation, which is the core issue at stake, can only be meaningfully explored if the picture is not clouded by another "pluri-" term that conceptually does not add anything. Pluricentricity is the model to work with until it is falsified.

I hope the points brought forth in this book will be meticulously scrutinized, tested and subjected to falsification from every possible angle. Whenever we describe language and its varieties, we need to ensure that our descriptions are not artefacts of our methods. As this chapter's epitaph shows, German singer Herbert Grönemeyer appreciates the differences between (Standard) Austrian German and (Standard) German German, as should all linguists unless they become, to use Weinreich et al.'s (1968: 179) term, "socially agnostic". It seems to me that "pluri-areality" represents just such agnosticism.

Notes

1 **Ronald Pohl:** Teilen Sie mit den Alpenrepublikanern die Vorliebe, sich "unpräzise" auszudrücken?
Herbert Grönemeyer: Was Sie als unpräzise beschreiben, ist der Spaß der Österreicher, mit der Sprache geschmeidig umzugehen. In Deutschland und speziell auch in Preußen betrachten wir die Sprache als Repräsentation unseres Ingenieurwesens.—Wir handhaben sie mit großer Präzision, neigen aber nicht dazu, ihr verspieltes Sentiment zu implantieren (www.derstandard.at/2000091364249/ Herbert-Groenemeyer-Warum-reagieren-wir-so-hochgescheucht, 14 Nov. 2018).
2 "verfügen nicht über die begriffliche Differenzierung zwischen Varietäten".

Bibliography

Agha, Asif. 2007. *Language and Social Relations*. New York: Cambridge University Press.

Albirini, Abdulkafi. 2016. *Modern Arabic Sociolinguisics*. London: Routledge.

Algeo, John. 2001. External history. In Algeo (ed.), 1–58.

Algeo, John (ed.). 2001. *The Cambridge History of the English Language. Vol. VI: English in North America*. Cambridge: CUP.

Ammon, Ulrich. 1995. *Die deutsche Sprache in Deutschland, Österreich und der Schweiz. Das Problem der nationalen Varietäten*. Berlin: Mouton de Gruyter.

Ammon, Ulrich et al. 2004. *Variantenwörterbuch des Deutschen*. 1st ed. Berlin: Mouton de Gruyter.

Ammon, Ulrich et al. 2016. *Variantenwörterbuch des Deutschen*. 2nd ed. Berlin: Mouton de Gruyter.

Anderson, Benedict. 2006. *Imagined Communities: Reflections on the Origins and Spread of Nationalism*. Rev. ed. London, UK: Verso.

Auer, Anita, Daniel Schreier and Richard J. Watts (eds.). 2015. *Letter Writing and Language Change*. Cambridge: CUP.

Auer, Peter. 2005. The construction of linguistic borders and the linguistic construction of borders. In Filppula et al. (eds.), 3–30.

Auer, Peter. 2011. Dialect vs. standard: A typology of scenarios in Europe. In *The Language and Linguistics of Europe: A Comprehensive Guide*, ed. by Bernd Kortmann and Johan van der Auwera, 485–500. Berlin: Mouton de Gruyter.

Auer, Peter. 2013. Enregistering pluricentric German. In *Pluricentricity: Language Variation and Sociocognitive Dimensions*, ed. by Augusto Soares Da Silva, 17–43. Berlin: De Grutyer.

Auer, Peter, Frans Hinskens and Paul Kerswill (eds.). 2005. *Dialect Change: Convergence and Divergence in European Languages*. Cambridge: CUP.

Avis, Walter S. 1954. Speech differences along the Ontario-United States border. I: Vocabulary. *Journal of the Canadian Linguistic Association* 1(1 October): 13–18.

Avis, Walter S. 1955. Speech differences along the Ontario–United States border. II: Grammar and syntax. *Journal of the Canadian Linguistic Association* 1(1 March): 14–19.

Avis, Walter S. 1956. Speech differences along the Ontario–United States border. III: Pronunciation. *Journal of the Canadian Linguistic Association* 2(1 March): 41–59.

Avis, Walter S. 1972. So *Eh?* is Canadian, Eh? *Canadian Journal of Linguistics* 17(2): 89–104.

Avis, Walter S. 1973. The English language in Canada In *Current trends in linguistics*. Vol. 10/1, ed. by Thomas Sebeok, 40–74. The Hague: Mouton.

Babel, Molly. 2010. Dialect convergence and divergence in New Zealand English. *Language in Society* 39(4): 437–456.

Bamgbose, Ayo. 1998. Torn between the norms: Innovations in World Englishes. *World Englishes* 17(1): 1–14.

Barbour, Stephen and Patrick Stevenson. 1990. *Variation in German: A Critical Approach to German Sociolinguistics*. Cambridge: CUP.

Bauer, Laurie and Peter Trudgill (eds.). 1998. *Language Myths*. London: Penguin.

Bednarek, Oldrich. 2017. *Sprachgebrauch und Sprachbeurteilung in Österreich am Beispiel der jüngeren Generation*. Berlin: Frank & Timme.

Belling, Luc and Julia de Bres. 2014. Digital superdiversity in Luxembourg the role of Luxembourgish in a multilingual Facebook group. *Discourse, Context and Media* 4–5: 74–85.

Berger, Christine M. 2005. The dialect topography of Canada: Method, coverage, interface and analyses. MA Thesis, University of Vienna.

Boberg, Charles. 2000. Geolinguistic diffusion and the U.S.-Canada border. *Language Variation and Change* 12: 1–24.

Boberg, Charles. 2005. The North American regional vocabulary survey: New variables and methods in the study of North American English. *American Speech* 80: 22–60.

Boberg, Charles. 2010. *The English Language in Canada: Status, History and Comparative Analysis*. Cambridge: CUP.

Brinton, Laurel J. and Margery Fee. 2001. Canadian English. In Algeo (ed.), 422–440.

Britain, David. 2002. Space and spatial diffusion. In *The Handbook of Language Variation and Change*, ed. by J. K. Chambers, Peter Trudgill and Natalie Schilling-Estes, 603–637. Malden, MA: Blackwell.

Britain, David. 2010. Conceptualizations of geographic space in linguistics. In *Language and Space: An International Handbook of Linguistic Variation. Vol. 2*, ed. by Peter Auer and Jürgen Erich Schmidt, 69–97. Berlin: Mouton de Gruyter.

Bruckmüller, Ernst. 1994. *Österreichbewusstsein im Wandel: Identität und Selbstverständnis in den 90er Jahren*. Vienna: Signum.

Burnett, Wendy. 2006. Linguistic resistance on the Maine–New Brunswick border. *Canadian Journal of Linguistics* 51(2/3): 161–176.

Cedergren, Henrietta J. 1973. The interplay of social and linguistic factors in Panama. Ph.D. dissertation, Cornell University.

Cerruti, Massimo, Claudia Crocco and Stefania Marzo (eds.). 2017. *Towards a New Standard: Theoretical and Empirical Studies on the Restandardization of Italian*. Berlin: Mouton De Gruyter.

Chambers, J. K. 1998. Social embedding of changes in progress. *Journal of English Linguistics* 26(1): 5–36.

Chambers, J. K. 2008. The tangled garden: Relics and vestiges in Canadian English. Focus on Canadian English, ed. Matthias Meyer. *Special Issue of Anglistik* 19: 7–21.

Chambers, J. K. 2009. *Sociolinguistic Theory*. 3rd rev. ed. Malden, MA: Wiley-Blackwell.

Chambers, J. K. 2010. English in Canada. In *Canadian English: A Linguistic Reader*, ed. by Elaine Gold and Janice McAlpine, 1–37. Kingston, ON: Strathy Language Unit. Online: http://www.queensu.ca/strathy/apps/OP6v2.pdf

Chambers, J. K. forthcoming. Borders and language. In *Processes of Change: Studies in Late Modern and Present-Day English*.

Chambers, J. K. and Peter Trudgill. 1998. *Dialectology*. 2nd ed. Cambridge: CUP.

Clyne, Michael G. 1984. *Language and Society in the German-speaking Countries*. Cambridge: CUP.

Clyne, Michael G. (ed.). 1992b. *Pluricentric Languages: Differing Norms in Different Nations*. Berlin: Mouton de Gruyter.

Clyne, Michael G. 1992a. Pluricentric languages—an introduction. In Clyne (ed.), 1–9.

Clyne, Michael G. 1995. *The German Language in a Changing Europe*. New York: CUP.

Considine, John. 2017. Parkade: One Canadianism or two Americanisms? *American Speech* 92(3): 281–297.

Coupland, Nikolas and Tore Kristiansen. 2011. SLICE: Critical perspectives on language (de)standardisation. In *Standard Languages and Language Standards in a Changing Europe*, ed. by Tore Kristiansen and Nikolas Coupland, 11–35. Oslo: Novus Press.

Crystal, David. 2017. The future of new Euro-Englishes. *World Englishes* 36(3): 330–335.

Daniel, Marcus. 2009. *Scandal and Civility: Journalism and the Birth of American Democracy*. Oxford: Oxford University Press.

Davies, Winifred V. 2009. Standard German in the nineteenth century. In Horan et al. (eds.), 189–210.

Davies, Winifred V., Annelies Häcki Buhofer, Regula Schmidlin, Melanie Wagner, Eva Lia Wyss (eds.). 2017. *Standardsprache zwischen Norm und Praxis: theoretische Betrachtungen, empirische Studien und sprachdidaktische Ausblicke*. Tübingen: Narr Frankce Attempto.

de Cillia, Rudolf. 1998. *Burenwurscht bleibt Burenwurscht. Sprache und gesellschaftliche Mehrsprachigkeit in Österreich*. Klagenfurt: Drava.

de Cillia, Rudolf. 2015. Deutsche Sprache und österreichische Identität/en. In Lenz et al., 149–164.

de Cillia, Rudolf. 2016. Konzeptualisierung der Variation des Deutschen in Österreich bei LehrerInnen und SchülerInnen: Ergebnisse aus einem Forschungsprojekt zum österreichischen Deutschals Unterrichts- und Bildungssprache. Paper read at the Conference "German in Austria", Vienna, July 2016.

de Cillia, Rudolf, Ilona E. Fink and Jutta Ransmayr. 2017. Varietäten des Deutschen and österreichischen Schulen. Ergebnisse des Forschungsprojekts Österreichisches Deutsch als Unterrichts- und Bildungssprache. In Davies et al. (eds.), 207–234.

de Cillia, Rudolf and Jutta Ransmayr. forthcoming. *Österreichisches Deutsch macht Schule?* Vienna: Böhlau.

Denis, Derek. 2013. The social meaning of *eh* in Canadian English. In *Proceedings of the 2013 Annual Conference of the Canadian Linguistics Association*, ed. by Shan Luo, 1–14. http://cla-acl.ca/actes-2013-proceedings/

Deumert, Ana and Wim Vandenbussche (eds.). 2003. *Germanic Standardizations: Past to Present*. Amsterdam: Benjamins.

Dollinger, Stefan. 2008. *New-Dialect Formation in Canada*. Amsterdam: Benjamins.

Dollinger, Stefan. 2010. Written sources of Canadian English: phonetic reconstruction and the low-back vowel merger In *Varieties in Writing: the Written Word as Linguistic Evidence*, ed. by Raymond Hickey, 197–222. Amsterdam: Benjamins.

Dollinger, Stefan. 2011. Academic and public attitudes to the notion of 'standard' Canadian English. *English Today* 27(4): 3–9. www.academia.edu/4049232/ (5 July 2018).

Dollinger, Stefan. 2012a. The western Canada-U.S. border as a linguistic boundary: The roles of L1 and L2 speakers. *World Englishes* 31(4): 519–533.

Dollinger, Stefan. 2012b. Standardvarietäten und Identität: Stand und Rezeption nationaler Wörterbücher in Österreich und Kanada. *tribüne* 3: 25–31.

Dollinger, Stefan. 2015a. *The Written Questionnaire in Social Dialectology: History, Theory, Practice*. Amsterdam: Benjamins.

Dollinger, Stefan. 2015b. How to write a historical dictionary: A sketch of the dictionary of Canadianisms on historical principles, Second Edition. *Ozwords* 24(2): 1–3, 6 (October). www.academia.edu/18967380/ (5 July 2018).

Dollinger, Stefan. 2016a. On parallels, differences and distortions in the pluricentricity of English and German. Paper Presented at the 2nd Deutsch in Österreich Conference, 7 July, Schönbrunn Castle. Franz Joseph's Lecture Hall. www.academia.edu/26828790/ (5 July 2018).

Dollinger, Stefan. 2016b. On the regrettable dichotomy between philology and linguistics: Historical lexicography and historical linguistics as test cases. In *Studies in the History of the English Language VII. Generalizing vs. Particularizing Methodologies in Historical Linguistic Analysis*, ed. by Don Chapman, Colette Moore and Miranda Wilcox Berlin: Mouton de Gruyter., 61–89. www.academia.edu/22416903/ (5 July 2018).

Dollinger, Stefan. 2016c. Googleology as smart lexicography: Big, messy data for better regional labels. *Dictionaries* 37: 60–98.

Dollinger, Stefan. 2017. TAKE UP #9 as a semantic isogloss on the Canada-US border. *World Englishes* 36(1): 80–103.

Dollinger, Stefan. 2019a. *Creating Canadian English: The Professor, the Mountaineer, and a National Variety of English*. Cambridge: CUP.

Dollinger, Stefan. 2019b. English in Canada. In *Handbook of World Englishes*. 2nd ed., ed. by Cecil Nelson, Zoya Proshina and Daniel Davis. Malden, MA: Blackwell-Wiley.

Dollinger, Stefan and Sandra Clarke. 2012. On the autonomy and homogeneity of Canadian English. *World Englishes* 31(4): 449–466.

Dollinger, Stefan (chief editor) and Margery Fee (associate editor). 2017. *DCHP-2: The Dictionary of Canadianisms on Historical Principles*. 2nd ed. With the assistance of Baillie Ford, Alexandra Gaylie and Gabrielle Lim. Vancouver: University of British Columbia. www.dchp.ca/dchp2

Dörnyei, Zoltán. 2003. *Questionnaires in Second Language Reserach: Construction, Administration, and Processing*. Mahwah, New Jersey: Erlbaum.

Dressler, Wolfgang U. 1997. Review of Ammon (1995). *Language in Society* 26(4): 608–611.

Durrell, Martin. 2002. Political unity and linguistic diversity in nineteenth-century Germany. In Umbach (ed.), 91–112.

Durrell, Martin. 2009. Deutsch: Teutons, Germans or Dutch? The problems of defining a nation. In Horan et al. (eds.), 167–188.

Durrell, Martin. 2017. Die Rolle der deutschen Sprache in ideologischen Konstrukten der Nation. In Davies et al. (eds.), 23–40.

Dürscheid, Christa. 2009. Variatio delectat? Die Plurizentrizität des Deutschen als Unterrichtsgegenstand. In *Deutsch unterrichten zwischen DaF, DaZ und DaM*, ed. by Monika Clalüna and Barbara Etterich, 59–69. Stallikon: AkDaF.

Dürscheid, Christa, Stephan Elspaß and Arne Ziegler. 2011. Grammatische Variabilität im Gebrauchsstandard: das Projekt "Variantengrammatik des Standarddeutschen". In *Grammatik und Korpora 2009: Dritte Internationale Konferenz*, ed. by Marek Konopka, Jacqueline Kubczak, Christian Mair, František Šticha and Ulrich H. Waßner, 123–140. Tübingen: Narr Francke Attempto.

Dürscheid, Christa and Stephan Elspaß. 2015. Variantengrammatik des Standarddeutschen. In *Regionale Variation des Deutschen—Projekte und Perspektiven*, ed. by Roland Kehrein, Alfred Lameli and Stefan Rabanus, 563–584. Berlin: Mouton de Gruyter.

Elspaß, Stephan and Christa Dürscheid. 2017. Areale grammatische variation in the Gebrauchsstandards des Deutschen. In *Grammatische Variation—empirische Zugänge und theoretische Modellierung*, ed. by Marek Konopka and Angelika Wöllstein, 85–104. Berlin: Mouton de Gruyter.

Elspaß, Stephan, Christa Dürscheid and Arne Ziegler. 2017. Zur grammatischen Pluriarealität der deutschen Gebrauchsstandards—oder: Über die Grenzen des Plurizentrizitätsbegriffs. In Sieburg and Solms (eds.), 69–91.

Elspaß, Stephan, Julia Engel and Konstantin Niehaus. 2013. Areale Variation in der Grammatik des Standarddeutschen - Problem oder Aufgabe? *gfl-journal* 2: 44–64.

Elspaß, Stephan and Konstantin Niehaus. 2014. The standardization of a modern pluriareal language. Concepts and corpus designs for German and beyond. *Orð og tunga* 16: 47–67.

Elspaß, Stephan, Nils Langer, Joachim Scharloth, Joachim and Wim Vandenbussche. 2007. *Germanic Language Histories 'from Below' (1700–2000)*. Berlin: Mouton de Gruyter (Studia Linguistica Germanica 86).

Embleton, Sheila, Dorin Uritescu and Eric S. Wheeler. 2013. Defining dialect regions with interpretations: Advancing the multidimensional scaling approach. *Literary and Linguistic Computing* 28(1): 13–20.

Filppula, Markku, Juhani Klemola, Marjatta Palander and Esa Penttilä (eds.). 2005. *Dialects Across Borders: Selected Papers from the 11th International Conference on Methods in Dialectology (Methods XI), Joensuu, August 2002*. Amsterdam: Benjamins.

Fisher, John Hurt. 2001. British and American, continuity and divergence. In Algeo (ed.), 59–85.

Gardt, Andreas (ed.). 2000. *Nation und Sprache: Die Diskussion ihrer Verhältnisses in Geschichte und Gegenwart*. Berlin: Mouton de Gruyter.

Ghyselen, Anne-Sophie, Steven Delarue and Chloé Lybaert. 2016. Studying standard language dynamics in Europe: Advances, issues & perspectives. *Taal en Tongval* 68(2): 75–91.

Gilles, Peter. 1999. *Dialektausgleich im Lëtzebuergeschen: Zur phonetisch-phonologischen Fokussierung einer Nationalsprache*. Tübingen: Niemeyer.

Gilles, Peter. 2000. Die Konstruktion einer Standardsprache: zur Koinédebatte in der Luxemburgischen Linguistik. In *Dialektologie zwischen Tradition und Neuansätzen*, ed. by Dieter Stellmacher, 200–212. Stuttgart: Steiner.

Gilles, Peter and Jürgen Trouvain. 2013. Luxembourgish. *Journal of the International Phonetic Association* 43(1): 67–74.

Glauninger, Manfred M. 2001. Zur Sonderstellung des Deutschen innerhalb der "plurizentrischen" Sprachen. Reflexionen anhand eines sprachgeschichtlichen Vergleichs zwischen Englisch und Deutsch, In *Sprache—Kultur—Indentiät. Festschrift für Katharina Wild zum 60. Geburtstag*, ed. by Peter Canisius, Zsuzsanna Gernr and Manfred M. Glauninger, 171–179. Pécs: University of Pécs.

Glauninger, Manfred M. 2013. Deutsch im 21. Jahrhundert: 'pluri-', 'supra-' oder 'postnational'? In *Im Dienste des Wortes: Lexikologische und lexikografische Streifzüge: Festschrift für Ioan Lazarescu*, ed. by Doris Sava and Hermann Scheuringer, 123–132. Passau: Stutz.

Goebl, Hans. 1984. *Dialektometrische Studien anhand italoromanischer, rätoromanischer und galloromanischer Sprachmaterialien aus ALS und ALF*. 3 vols. Tübingen: Niemeyer.

Goebl, Hans. 2007. A bunch of dialectometric flowers: A brief introduction to dialectometry. In Smit et al. (eds.), 133–172.

Gold, Elaine and Mireille Tremblay. 2006. *Eh?* and *Hein?*: Discourse particles or national icons? *Canadian Journal of Linguistics* 51(2&3): 247–264.

Grieve, Jack. 2016. *Regional Variation in Written American English*. Cambridge: CUP.

Grondelaers, Stefan and Roeland van Hout. 2011. The Standard language situation in the Low Countries: Top-down and bottom-up variations on a diaglossic theme. *Journal of Germanic Linguistics* 23(3): 199–243.

Grondelaers, Stefan, Roeland van Hout and Paul van Gent. 2016. Destandardization is not destandardization: Revising standardness criteria in order to revisit standard language typologies in the Low Countries. *Taal en Tongval* 68(2): 119–149.

Haas, Willy. 1969. Zur Einführung. In *Franz Werfel: Eine Auslese*, ed. by Ruth Stadelmann, 7–16. Wien and Heidelberg: Ueberreuter.

Haspelmath, Martin. 2019. How comparative concepts and descriptive linguistic categories are different. In *Aspects of Linguistic Variation*, ed. by Daniel Olmen, Tanja Mortelmans and Frank Brisard, 83–114. Berlin: Mouton de Gruyter.

Haugen, Einar. 1966. *Language Conflict and Language Planning: The Case of Modern Norwegian*. Cambridge: Harvard University Press.

Havinga Anna D. 2018. *Invisibilising Austrian German: On the Effect of Linguistic Prescriptions and Educational Reforms on Writing Practices in 18th-century Austria*. Berlin: Mouton de Gruyter.

Herrgen, Joachim. 2015. Entnationalisierung des Standards. Eine perzeptionslinguistische Untersuchung zur deutschen Standardsprache in Deutschland, Österreich und der Schweiz. In Lenz and Glauninger (2015), 139–164.

Hickey, Raymond. 2012. Standard English and standards of English. In *Standards of English. Codified Varieties Around the World,* ed. by R. Hickey. Cambridge: CUP.

Hickey, Raymond. 2017. Areas, areal features and reality. In the Germanic languages and areal linguistics. In *The Cambridge Handbook of Areal Linguistics,* ed. by Raymond Hickey, 1–15. Cambridge: CUP.

Hinskens, Frans. 1993. Dialekt als lingua franca? Dialektgebruik in het algemeen en bij grensoverschijdend contact in het Nederrijnland en Twenet. In Kremer (ed.), 209–245.

Hinskens, Frans, Peter Auer and Paul Kerswill. 2005. The study of dialect convergence and divergence: Conceptual and methodological considerations. In Auer et al. (eds.), 1–48.

Hobel, Bettina, Sylvia Moosmüller and Christian Kaseß. The phonetic realisation of orthographic <ä, äh> in Standard Austrian German. Paper Presented at the 2nd Deutsch in Österreich Conference, Schönbrunn Castle (8 July 2016).

Horan, Geraldine, Nils Langer and Sheila Watts (eds.). 2009. *Landmarks in the History of the German Language.* Oxford. Lang.

Horner, Kristine. 2005. Reimagining the nation: Discourses of language purism in Luxembourg. In Langer and Davies (eds.), 166–185.

Hrauda, Carl Friedrich. 1948. *Die Sprache des Österreichers.* Salzburg: Österreichischer Kulturverlag.

Jahr, Ernst Håkon. 2003. Norwegian. In Deumert and Vandenbussche (eds.), 331–354.

Jenkins, Jennifer. 2007. *English as a Lingua Franca: Attitude and Identity.* Oxford: Oxford University Press.

Johnstone, Barbara. 2011. Dialect enregisterment in performance. *Journal of Sociolinguistics* 15(5): 657–679.

Kachru, Braj. 1985. Standards, codification and sociolinguistic realism: The English language in the Outer Circle. In *English in the World: Teaching and Learning of Language and Literature*, ed. by Randolph Quirk and Henry G. Widdowson, 11–36. Cambridge: CUP.

Kellermeier-Rehbein, Birte. 2014. *Plurizentrik: Einführung in die nationalen Varietäten des Deutschen.* Berlin: Erich Schmidt Verlag.

Kerswill, Paul. 1994. *Dialects Converging: Rural Speech in Urban Norway.* Oxford: Clarendon Press.

Kircher, Ruth. 2012. How pluricentric is the French language? An investigation of attitudes towards Quebec French compared to European French. *Journal of French Language Studies* 22(3): 345–370.

Kloss, Heinz. 1952. *Die Entwicklung neuer germanischer Kultursprachen von 1800 bis 1950.* Munich: Pohl & Co.

Kloss, Heinz. 1967. 'Abstand languages' and 'Ausbau languages'. *Anthropological Linguistics* 9(7): 29–41.

Kloss, Heinz. 1978. *Die Entwicklung neuer germanischer Kultursprachen seit 1800.* 2nd ed. Düsseldorf: Schwann.

Kloss, Heinz. 1993. Abstand Languages and Ausbau Languages. *Anthropological Linguistics* 35(1/4): 158–170.

Koppensteiner, Wolfgang and Alexandra N. Lenz. 2016. Looking for a standard— Austrian Perspectives. Paper Presented at the 2nd Deutsch in Österreich Conference, 7 July, Schönbrunn Castle, Vienna.

Koppensteiner, Wolfgang and Alexandra N. Lenz. 2017. Theoretische und methodische Herausforderungen einer perzeptiv-attitudinalen Standardsprachenforschung. Perspektiven aus und auf Österreich. In Sieburg and Solms (eds.), 43–68.

Kortmann, Bernd, Kate Burridge, Rajend Mesthrie, Edgar W. Schneider and Clive Upton (eds.). 2004. *A Handbook of Varieties of English. Vol. II: Morphology and Syntax*. Berlin: Mouton de Gruyter.

Kortmann, Bernd and Kerstin Luckenheimer (eds.). 2011. *The Electronic World Atlas of Varieties of English* [eWAVE]. Leipzig: Max Planck Institute for Evolutionary Anthropology. www.ewave-atlas.org

Krassnig, Albert. 1958. Das Österreichische Wörterbuch. *Muttersprache* 68: 155–157.

Kremer, Ludger. 1979. *Grenzmundarten und Mundartgrenzen*. Köln: Böhlau.

Kremer, Ludger (ed.). 1993. *Diglossiestudien: Dialekt und Standardsprache im niederländisch-deutschen Grenzland*. Vreden: Landeskundliches Institut Westmünsterland.

Kretzschmar, William A. Jr. 2008. Standard American English pronunciation. In *Varieties of English. Vol. 2: The Americas and the Caribbean*, ed. by Edgar W. Schneider, 37–51. Berlin: Mouton de Gruyter.

Küpper, Achim, Torsten Leuschner and Björn Rothstein. 2017. Die deutschsprachige Gemeinschaft Belgiens als emergentes Zentrum. Sprach- und bildungspolitischer Kontext—(Sub-)Standard—Sprachlandschaft. In Sieburg and Solms (eds.), 169–192.

Labov, William. 1994. *Principles of Linguistic Change. Vol. 1: Internal Factors*. Oxford: Blackwell.

Labov, William. 2001. *Principles of Linguistic Change. Vol. 2: Social Factors*. Oxford: Blackwell.

Labov, William. 2003. Pursuing the cascade model. In *Social dialectology: In honour of Peter Trudgill*, ed. by David Britain and Jenny Cheshire, 9–22. Amsterdam: Benjamins.

Labov, William. 2010. *Principles of Linguistic Changes. Vol. 3: Cognitive and Cultural Factors*. Chichester: Blackwell-Wiley.

Labov, William, Sharon Ash and Charles Boberg. 2005. *The Atlas of North American English. Phonetics, Phonology and Sound Change*. Berlin: Mouton de Gruyter.

Langer, Nils and Winifred V. Davies (eds.). 2005. *Linguistic Purism in the Germanic Languages*. Berlin: Mouton de Gruyter.

Lenz, Alexandra N. 2018. The special research programme "German in Austria. Variation—contact—perception". In *Language Choice in Tourism—Focus on Europe*, 269–277. Berlin: Mouton de Gruyter.

Lenz, Alexandra N. and Manfred Glauninger. 2015. *Standarddeutsch im 21. Jahrhundert: Theoretische und Empirische Ansätze mit einem Fokus auf Österreich*. Wuppertal: V&R unipress.

Lenz, Alexandra N., Charlotte Gooskens and Siemon Reker (eds.). 2009. *Niedersächsische Dialekte über Grenzen hinweg*. Stuttgart: Steiner.

Lenz, Alexandra N., Timo Ahlers and Manfred M. Glauninger (eds.). 2015. *Dimensionen des Deutschen in Österreich: Variation und Varietäten im sozialen Kontext*. Frankfurt and Main: Lang.

Llamas, Carmen, Dominic Watt and Daniel Ezra Johnson. 2009. Linguistic accommodation and the salience of national identity markers in a border town. *Journal of Language and Social Psychology* 28(4): 381–407.

Lybaert, Chloé. 2017. A direct discourse-based approach to the study of language attitudes: The case of *tussentaal* in Flanders. *Language Sciences* 59: 93–116.

Maas, Utz. 2014. *Was ist deutsch? Die Entwicklung der sprachlichen Verhältnisse in Deutschland*, 2. überarbeitete Auflage. Stuttgart: UTB-Band.

Matras, Yaron. 2015. Transnational policy and 'authenticity' discourses on Romani language and identity. *Language in Society* 44. 295–316.

Mattheier, Klaus. 1997. Über Destandardisierung, Umstandardisierung und Standardisierung in modernen europäischen Standardsprachen. In *Standardisierung und Destandardisierung europäischer Nationalsprachen*, ed. by Klaus Mattheier and Edgar Radtke, 1–9. Frankfurt: Lang.

Mattheier, Klaus. 2003. German. In Deumert & Vandenbussche (eds.), 211–244.

McColl Millar, Robert. 2005. *Language, Nation and Power: An Introduction*. London: Palgrave Macmillan.

Mencken, Henry L. 1936. *The American Language*. 4th ed. New York: Knopf.

Mendes, Amália, Maria Eugênia Lammoglia Duarte, Maria Fernanda Bacelar do Nascimento, Luísa Pereira and Antónia Estrela. 2014. Pronominal constructions and subject indetermination in national varieties of Portuguese—a global view on norms. In Muhr and Marley (2014), 101–116.

Moosmüller, Sylvia, C. Schmid and J. Brandstätter. 2015. Standard Austrian German. *Journal of the International Phonetic Association* 45(3): 339–348.

Moosmüller, Sylvia. 1991. *Hochsprache und Dialekt in Österreich: soziophonetische Untersuchungen zu ihrer Abgrenzung in Wien, Graz, Salzburg und Innsbruck*. Vienna: Böhlau.

Muhr, Rudolf. 1983. Über das Für und Wider der Kritik am Österreichischen Wörterbuch. *Informationen zur Deutschdidaktik* 8(4): 134–138.

Muhr, Rudolf. 1989. Deutsch und Österreich(isch): Gespaltene Sprache—Gespaltenes Bewusstsein—Gespaltene Identität. *ide (Informationen zur Deutschdidaktik) (Klagenfurt)* 2(13th year): 74–98.

Muhr, Rudolf. 1995. Österreichisches Deutsch: Linguistische, sozialpsychologische und sprachpolitische Aspekte einer nationalen Variante des Deutschen. In Muhr, Schrodt and Wiesinger (eds.), 75–109.

Muhr, Rudolf. 1996. Österreichisches deutsch—nationalismus? Einige argument wider den zeitgeist—Eine klarstellung. *tribüne: zeitschrift fur sprache und schreibung* 1: 12–18.

Muhr, Rudolf. 2003. Language change via satellite: The influence of German television broadcasting on Austrian German. *Journal of Historical Pragmatics* 4: 103–127.

Muhr, Rudolf. 2007. Österrreichisches Aussprachewörterbuch—Österreichische Aussprachedatenbank. Frankfurt/Main: Lang. www.adaba.at.

Muhr, Rudolf. 2012. *Non-dominant Varieties of Pluricentric Languages: Getting the Picture. In Memory of Michael Clyne*. In Collaboration with Catrin Norrby, Leo Kretzenbacher and Carla Amorós. Frankfurt: Peter.

Muhr, Rudolf (ed.). 2016a. *Pluricentric Languages and Non-Dominant Varieties Worldwide. Part I: Pluricentric Languages across Continents. Features and Usage.* Frankfurt: Peter Lang.

Muhr, Rudolf (ed.). 2016b. *Pluricentric Languages and Non-Dominant Varieties Worldwide. Part II: The Pluricentricity of Portuguese and Spanish. New Concepts and Descriptions.* Frankfurt: Peter Lang.

Muhr, Rudolf. 2017. Das Österreichische Deutsch. In Sieburg and Solms (eds.), 23–41. Lang.

Muhr, Rudolf and Dawn Marley (eds.). 2015. *Pluricentric Languages: New Perspective in Theory and Description.* Frankfurt/Main: Lang.

Muhr, Rudolf and Richard Schrodt (eds.). 1997. *Österreichisches Deutsch und andere nationale Varietäten plurizentrischer Sprachen in Europa.* Wien: HPT.

Muhr, Rudolf, Richard Schrodt and Peter Wiesinger (eds.). 1995. *Österreichisches Deutsch: Linguistische, sozialpsychologische und sprachpolitische Aspekte einer nationalen Variante des Deutschen.* Wien: HPT.

Nerbonne, John. 2015. Review of Pickl (2013). *Zeitschrift für Rezensionen zur germanistischen Sprachwissenschaft* 7(1&2): 124–129.

New, William H. 1998. *Borderlands: How We Talk About Canada.* Vancouver: UBC Press.

Niehaus, Konstantin. 2017. Die Begrenztheit plurizentrisicher Grenzen: grammatische Variation in der pluriarealen Sprache Deutsch. In Davies et al. (eds.), 61–88.

Owens, Thompson W. and Paul M. Baker. 1984. Linguistic insecurity in Winnipeg: Validation of a Canadian index of linguistic insecurity. *Language in Society* 13: 337–350.

Paffey, Darren 2012. *Language Ideologies and the Globalization of Standard Spanish.* London: Bloomsbury.

Partridge, Eric and John W. Clark (eds.). 1951. *British and American English Since 1900. With Contributions on English in Canada, South Africa, Australia, New Zealand and India.* New York: Greenwood Press.

Pedersen, Inge Lise. 2005. Processes of standardisation in Scandinavia. In Auer, Hinskens and Kerswill (eds.), 171–195.

Peter, Klaus. 2015. Sprachliche Normvorstellungen in Österreich, Deutschland und der Schweiz. In Lenz, Ahlers and Glauninger (eds.), 123–147.

Pfrehm, James W. 2007. An empirical study of the pluricentricity of German: Comparing German and Austrian nationals' perceptions of the use, pleasantness, and standardness of Austrian Standard and German Standard lexical items. PhD dissertation, University of Wisconsin, Madison.

Pickl, Simon. 2013. *Probabilistische Geolinguistik. Geostatistische Analysen lexikalischer Variation in Bayerisch-Schwaben.* Stuttgart: Steiner.

Pickl, Simon, Aaron Spettl, Simon Pröll, Stephan Elspaß, Werner König and Volker Schmidt. 2014. Linguistic distances in dialectometric intensity estimation. *Journal of Linguistic Geography* 2: 25–40.

Pohl, Heinz Dieter. 1997. Gedanken zum Österreichischen Deutsch (als Teil der "pluriarealen" deutschen Sprache). In Muhr and Schrodt (eds.), 67–88.

Pohl, Heinz. 2017. Anglizismen—Austriazismen. *Wiener Sprachblätter* 67(3 September): 40.

Pohl, Heinz. 2018. Die deutsche Sprache in Österreich: von den Dialekten zur landestypischen Standardisierung. *Sprachspiegel* 74(5): 130–142.

Polenz, Peter von. 1999. *Deutsche Sprachgeschichte vom Spaätmittelalter bis zur Gegenwart. Bd. 3. 19. und 20. Jahrhundert.* Berlin: Mouton de Gruyter.

Popper, Karl R. 1966 [1934]. Logik der Forschung. Zweite, erw. Auflage. Tübingen: Mohr.

Preston, Dennis. 1998. They speak really bad English down south and in New York City. In Bauer and Trudgill (eds.), 139–149.

Quirk, Randolph, Sidney Greenbaum, Geoffrey Leech and Jan Svartvik. 1985. *A Comprehensive Grammar of the English Language.* London: Longman.

Ransmayr, Jutta. 2006. *Der Status des Österreichischen Deutsch an Auslandsuniversitäten. Eine empirische Untersuchung.* Frankfurt: Lang.

Ransmayr, Jutta. 2016. Insiders' and outsiders' views on German from Austria's perspective. Austrian Standard German and German Standard German—the odd couple. *EFNIL Conference* 2016, Warsaw (20 September).

Ransmayr, Jutta. 2018. Austrian media corpus. In *Germanistik Digital,* ed. by Ingo Börner, Wolfgang Straub and Christian Zolles, 168–182. Vienna: Facultas.

Ransmayr, Jutta, Karlheinz Mörth and Matej Ďurčo. 2017. AMC (Austrian Media Corpus)—Korpusbasierte Forschungen zum Österreichischen Deutsch. In *Digitale Methoden der Korpusforschung in Österreich,* ed. by Claudia Resch and Wolfgang U. Dressler, 27–38. Vienna: Verlag der Österreichischen Akademie der Wissenschaften.

Rice, Keren and Leslie Saxon. 2002. Issues of standardization and community in Aboriginal language lexicography. In *Making Dictionaries: Preserving Indigenous Languages of the Americas,* ed. by William Frawley, Kenneth C. Hill and Pamela Munro, 125–154. Berkeley: University of California Press.

Romaine, Suzanne. 1988. Historical sociolinguistics: problems and methodology. In *Sociolinguistics/Soziolinguistik: An international handbook of the science of language and society,* ed. by Ulrich Ammon, Norbert Dittmar, Klaus J. Mattheier & Peter Trudgill, II: 1452–1468. Berlin: de Gruyter.

Ruette, Tom and Dirk Speelman. 2014. Transparent aggregation of variables with Individual Differences Scaling. *Literary and Linguistic Computing* 29(1): 89–106.

Sadlier-Brown, Emily. 2012. Across the country, across the border: Homogeneity and autonomy of Canadian Raising. *World Englishes* 31(4): 534–548. Special issue on "Canadian English: Autonomy and Homogeneity" ed. by Stefan Dollinger and Sandra Clarke.

Scanavino, Chiara. 2015. *Deutschlandismen in den Lernerwörterbüchern.* Frankfurt: Peter Lang.

Scheichl, Sigurd Paul. 1996. Konnte Grillparzer deutsch? Gedanken zu einer Geschichte der deutschen Literatursprache in Österreich seit 1800. *Jahrbuch der Grillparzer Gesellschaft* 3/19: 147–169.

Scheuringer, Hermann. 1985. The state border as a dialect border—on the necessity of dialect geography in dialectology. In Warkentyne (ed.). *Papers from the Fifth International Conference on Methods in Dialectology,* 443–455. Victoria: University of Victoria.

ScheuringerHermann. 1990a. *Sprachentwicklung in Bayern und Österreich. Eine Analyse des Substandardverhaltens der Städte Braunau am Inn (Österreich) und Simbach am Inn (Bayern) und ihres Umlandes.* Hamburg: Buske.

Scheuringer, Hermann1990b. Bayerisches Bairisch und österreichisches Bairisch. Die deutsch-österreichische Staatsgrenze als Sprachgrenze? In *Grenzdialekte: Studien zur Entwicklung kontinentalwestgermanischer Dialektkontinua,* ed. by Ludger Kremer and Hermann Niebaum. Hildesheim, 361–381.

Scheuringer, Hermann. 1996. Das Deutsche als pluriareale Sprache: ein Beitrag gegen staatlich begrenzte Horizonte in der Diskussion um die deutsche Sprache in Österreich. *Die Unterrichtspraxis* 29(2): 147–153.

Scheuringer, Hermann. 1997. Sprachvarietäten in Österreich. In *Varietäten des Deutschen: Regional- und Umgangssprachen*, ed. by Gerhard Stickel, 332–345. Berlin: Mouton de Gruyter.

Schmidlin, Regula. 2011. *Die Vielfalt des Deutschen: Standard und Variation. Gebrauch, Einschätzung und Kodifizierung einer Plurizentrischen Sprache.* Berlin: Mouton de Gruyter.

Schmidlin, Regula. 2017. Diglossie und Plurizentrik: Ergebnisse und Perspektiven zum Sprachgebrauch in der Deutschschweiz. In Sieburg and Solms (eds.), 93–106.

Schmidlin, Regula, Eva L. Wyss and Winifred V. Davies. 2017. Plurizentrik revisited—aktuelle Perspektiven auf die Variation der detuschen Standardsprache. In Davies et al. (eds.), 7–20.

Schmidt-Dengler, Wendelin. 1995. Vom Staat, der keiner war, zur Literatur, die keine ist. Zur Leidensgeschichte der österreichischen Literaturgeschichte. In Muhr, Schrodt and Wiesinger (eds.), 38–52.

Schmidt, Jürgen Erich and Joachim Herrgen. 2011. *Sprachdynamik: Eine Einführung in die moderne Regionalsprachenforschung.* Berlin: Erich Schmidt.

Schneider, Edgar W. 2007. *Postcolonial English: Varieties Around the World.* Cambridge: CUP.

Schneider, Edgar W., Kate Burridge, Bernd Kortmann, Rajend Mesthrie and Clive Upton (eds.). 2004. *A Handbook of Varieties of English. Vol. I: Phonology.* Berlin: Mouton de Gruyter.

Schrodt, Richard. 1997. Nationale Varianten, areale Unterschiede und der "Substandard": An den Quellen des Österreichischen Deutsch. In Muhr and Schrodt, 12–39.

Schrodt, Richard. 2012. Über Händl Klaus' Stücke *Ich ersehne die Alpen* und *So entstehen die Seen.* In *Jelinek[Jahr]Buch 3*, ed. by Pia Janke, 256–263. Vienna: Praesens.

Seidlhofer, Barbara. 2007. English as a lingua franca and communities of practice. In *Anglistentag 2006 Halle: Proceedings*, ed. by S. Volk-Birke and J. Lippert, 307–318. Trier: Wissenschaftlicher Verlag.

Seidlhofer, Barbara and Henry Widdowson. 2017. Thoughts on independent English. *World Englishes* 36(3): 360–362.

Seifter, Thorsten and Ingolf Seifter. 2016. Wir gegen uns: das "österreichische Deutsh" im Klassenzimmer—und der regio-normative Ausweg. *Beiträge zur Fremdsprachenvermittlung* 57: 39–60.

Segev, Tom. 2018. Interview with Renata Schmidtkunz on 17 May, Ö1 radio, Austria, c. minute 39–41. https://oe1.orf.at/player/20180517/513770

Sieburg, Heinz. 2017. "Luxemburger Standarddeutsch?" Hintergründe und Perspektiven. In Sieburg and Solms (eds.), 125–143.

Sieburg, Heinz and Hans-Joachim Solms (eds.). 2017. *Das Deutsche als plurizentrische Sprache: Ansprüche—Ergebnisse—Perspektiven.* Berlin: Erich Schmidt Verlag.

Smit, Ute, Stefan Dollinger, Julia Hüttner, Gunter Kaltenböck, Ursula Lutzky (eds.). 2007. *Tracing English through Time: Explorations in Language Variation.* Vienna: Braumüller.

Soukup, Barbara. 2013. The measurement of "language attitudes": A reappraisal from a constructionist perspective. In *Language (de)standardisation in Late Modern Europe: Experimental Studies,* ed. by Stefan Grondelaers & Tore Kristiansen, 251–66. Oslo: Novus Press.

Soukup, Barbara. 2016. Doing 'speaking the (non-)standard' in the media. *Taal et Tongval* 68(2): 151–172.

Stemberger, Katharina. 2018. *Katharina Stemberger—Im Gespräch* mit Renata Schmidtkunz, Ö1 radio, ORF. Vienna, aired 26 April 2018, 21:00–21:55 (at c21:49). https://oe1.orf.at/player/20180426/511184 (2 May 2018).

Sutter, Patrizia. 2017. *Diatopische Variation im Wörterbuch: Theorie und Praxis.* Berlin: Mouton de Gruyter.

Trudgill, Peter. 1974. Linguistic change and diffusion: Description and explanation in sociolinguistic dialect Geography. *Language in Society* 2: 215–246.

Trudgill, Peter. 1986. *Dialects in Contact.* Oxford: Blackwell.

Trudgill, Peter. 2000. *Sociolinguistics: An Introduction to Language and Society.* 4th ed. [1st ed. 1974]. Harmondsworth: Penguin.

Trudgill, Peter. 2004. *New-Dialect Formation: The Inevitability of Colonial Englishes.* Edinburgh: Edinburgh University Press.

Trudgill, Peter. 2011. *Sociolinguistic Typology: Social Determinants of Linguistic Complexity.* Oxford: Oxford University Press.

Trudgill, Peter. 2018. Address to the UBC Convocation. Honorary address read on the occasion of receiving a Dr. h.c. from UBC Vancouver, 30 November, Chan Centre of the Performing Arts.

Umbach, Maiken (ed.). 2002. *German Federalism: Past, Present, Future.* Houndmills: Palgrave.

Vandenbussche, Wim. 2011. Standardisation through the media: The case of Dutch in Flanders. In *Variatio Delectat: Empirische Evidenzen und theoretische Passungen sprachlicher Variation,* ed. by Peter Gilles, Joachim Scharloth and Evelyn Ziegler, 309–322. Frankfurt: Lang.

Van der Auwera, Johan and Daniel Van Olmen. 2017. The Germanic languages and areal linguistics. In *The Cambridge Handbook of Areal Linguistics,* ed. by Raymond Hickey, 239–269. Cambridge: CUP.

Warkentyne, Henry J. 1983. Attitudes and language behavior. *Canadian Journal of Linguistics* 28: 71–76.

Warkentyne, Henry J. (ed.). 1985. *Methods/Méthodes V. 1984.* Victoria, B.C.: University of Victoria.

Watt, Dominic, Carmen Llamas, and Daniel Ezra Johnson. 2010. Levels of linguistic accommodation across a national border. *Journal of English Linguistics* 38(3): 270–289.

Watt, Dominic and Carmen Llamas (ed.). 2014. *Language, Borders and Identity*. Edinburgh: Edinburgh University Press.

Watts, Richard and Peter Trudgill (eds.). 2002. *Alternative Histories of English*. London: Routledge.

Weinreich, Uriel. 1954. *Languages in Contact*. The Hague: Mouton.

Weinreich, Uriel, William Labov and Marvin Herzog. 1968. Empirical foundations for a theory of language change. In *Directions in Historical Linguistics*, ed. by Winfried P. Lehmann and Yakov Malkiel, 95–195. Austin, TX: University of Texas Press.

Whaley, Joachim. 2002. Federal habits; the Holy Roman Empire and the continuity of German federalism. In Umbach (ed.), 15–41.

Widdowson, Henry G. 1994. The ownership of English. *TESOL Quarterly* 28(2): 377–389.

Wiesinger, Peter. 2000. *Nation* und *Sprache* in Österreich. In Gardt (2000), 525–562.

Wiesinger, Peter. 2006. Zum Österreichischen Wörterbuch: aus Anlaß der 38. neubearbeiteten Auflage (1997). In *Das Österreichische Deutsch*, ed. by Peter Wiesinger, 177–201. Wien: Böhlau.

Wiesinger, Peter. 2014. *Das österreichische Deutsch in Gegenwart und Geschichte*. 3. aktualisierte und neuerlich erweiterte Auflage. Berlin: LitVerlag.

Wittgenstein, Ludwig. 1926. *Wörterbuch für Volksschulen*. Ed. by Adolf Hübner et al. Wien: HPT.

Wodak, Ruth, Rudolf de Cillia, Martin Reisigl and Karin Liebhart. 2009. *The Discursive Construction of National Identity*. 2nd ed. Edinburgh: Edinburg University Press.

Wolf, Norbert. 2012. Die deutsche Sprache im Zeitalter der Globalisierung. *Neuphilologische Mitteilungen* 113(4): 497–509.

Wolf, Norbert. 1994. Österreichisches zum Österreichischen Deutsch. *Zeitschrift für Dialektologie und Linguistik* 61(1): 66–76.

Wollmann, Franz. 1948. Die Sprache des Österreichers. *Erziehung und Unterricht* 7/8: 345–366.

Woolhiser, Curt. 2011. Border effects and European dialect continua: Dialect divergence and convergence. In *The Language and Linguistics of Europe: A Comprehensive Guide*, ed. by Bernd Kortmann and Johan van der Auwera, 501–523. Berlin: Mouton de Gruyter.

Zehetner, Ludwig. 1995. Review of Scheuringer (1990a). *Zeitschrift für Dialektolgoie und Linguistik* 62(3): 354–357.

Index